ARCHITECTURAL DESIGN

CW00816308

EDITORIAL OFFICES:
42 LEINSTER GARDENS, LONDON W2 3AN
TEL: + 44 171 262 5097 FAX: + 44 171 262 5093

EDITOR: Maggie Toy
DEPUTY EDITOR: Ellie Duffy
DESIGN: Mario Bettella and Andrea Bettella / Artmedia
ADVERTISEMENT SALES: Nicky Douglas

CONSULTANTS: Catherine Cooke, Terry Farrell, Kenneth Frampton, Charles Jencks, Heinrich Klotz, Leon Krier, Robert Maxwell, Demetri Porphyrios, Kenneth Powell, Colin Rowe, Derek Walker

SUBSCRIPTION OFFICES:

UK: JOHN WILEY & SONS LTD
JOURNALS ADMINISTRATION DEPARTMENT
1 OAKLANDS WAY, BOGNOR REGIS
WEST SUSSEX, PO22 9SA, UK
TEL: 01243 843272 FAX: 01243 843232
E-mail: cs-journals@wiley.co.uk

USA AND CANADA:
JOHN WILEY & SONS, INC
JOURNALS ADMINISTRATION DEPARTMENT
605 THIRD AVENUE
NEW YORK, NY 10158
TEL: + 1 212 850 6645 FAX: + 1 212 850 6021
CABLE JONWILE TELEX: 12-7063
E-mail: subinfo@wiley.com

ANNUAL SUBSCRIPTION RATES 1998: **UK** £90.00, *student rate*: £65.00; **Outside UK** US$145.00, *student rate*: $105.00. *AD* is published six times a year. Prices are for six issues and include postage and handling charges. Periodicals postage paid at Jamaica, NY 11431. Air freight and mailing in the USA by Publications Expediting Services Inc, 200 Meacham Ave, Elmont, Long Island, NY 11003.

SINGLE ISSUES: **UK** £18.99; **Outside UK** $29.95. Order two or more titles and postage is free. For orders of one title please add £2.00/$5.00. To receive order by air please add £5.50/$10.00.

POSTMASTER: send address changes to AD, c/o Publications Expediting Services Inc, 200 Meacham Ave, Elmont, Long Island, NY 11003.

Printed in Italy. All prices are subject to change without notice. [ISSN: 0003-8504]

CONTENTS

ARCHITECTURAL DESIGN **MAGAZINE**

HGA, Plains Art Museum, Fargo, North Dakota

ARCHITECTURAL DESIGN **PROFILE** NO 134

THE EVERYDAY AND ARCHITECTURE

Sarah Wigglesworth *and* **Jeremy Till** • *The (Extra)ordinary* • **Greil Marcus** • *Nicholas Till* • **Susan Nigra Snyder** *and* **Alex Wall** • *Patrick Keiller* • **Gillian Horn** • *Making the Everyday* • **Phillip Hall-Patch** • *Michael Marriott* • **Níall McLaughlin** • *Ben Kelly Design* • **Åsmund Thorkildsen** • *Jessica Stockholder* • **Using the Everyday** • *Katharina Ledersteger-Goodfriend* • **Rewi Thompson** • *Clark Stevens* • **Samuel Mockbee** • *Le K Architectures* • **Günter Behnisch**

Rasem Badran, Museum of Islamic Arts, Quatar

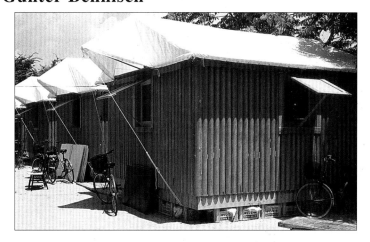

Shigeru Ban, Paper Log houses, Kobe, Japan

HAMMEL GREEN & ABRAHAMSON (HGA)

PLAINS ART MUSEUM
Fargo, North Dakota

The Plains Art Museum opened in October 1997 in a turn-of-the-century warehouse building that was renovated to house a permanent collection. This consists of over 2,000 pieces of regional art, traditional American Indian art, contemporary art and traditional folk art.

Although much of the building core was removed, the architects left the exterior fabric of the warehouse intact as well as the rough-hewn wood floors and large double-hung windows, before inserting four storeys of modern technology.

The space is designed to be as flexible as possible. The building comprises 56,000 square feet in total, with 9,000 square feet set aside for exhibition space. The exhibits are arranged over three levels. According to the project architect, the greatest challenge posed by the historic building was, 'to take a historical building, with very little heat and humidity control, and create within it a highly controllable core for storage, prep and gallery space'. However, the architects were well-acquainted with museum design, having worked on the Minnesota History Center, the Walker Arts Center and the recent gallery remodelling of the Minneapolis Institute of Arts.

The new facility accommodates an area for performance art, a resource library and, as is customary for today's museum, a restaurant and a gift shop. Ancillary areas are screened off discreetly, maintaining the uniform nature of the structure.

The essence of the interior is reinforced by the limited palette of colour and materials which provides a suitable backdrop for the everchanging range of exhibits. The fluid space is illuminated by artificial means and by natural light, which is admitted through the central skylight and the large windows. This is carefully filtered in order to avoid the harmful effect of ultra-violet rays.

BELOW, L TO R: Site plan; first floor plan; section

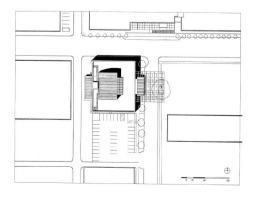

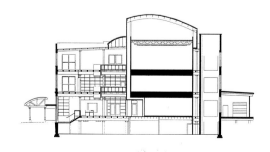

IV

MUSEUM OF ISLAMIC ARTS

INTERNATIONAL ARCHITECTURAL COMPETITION
Doha, Qatar

The competition to design a new museum in Doha was coordinated by the Aga Khan Trust for Culture in Geneva. In addition to housing four galleries (paintings and engravings; rare books, maps, prints and manuscripts; numismatics; weapons and armaments), the Museum of Islamic Arts aims to provide educational and research facilities.

The selection of international practices came from a shortlist of 81 responses to a public announcement. Here, *AD* features the winning design by Rasem Badran and four of the proposals. Included in the shortlist were Charles Correa (India), Zaha Hadid (Iraq/UK), Richard Rogers (UK) and James Wines (USA), and Oriol Bohigas (Spain).

An independent jury was also appointed to assess the submitted entries, reviewing each project on the basis of its strengths, weaknesses, and conformity to the competition requirements. This consisted of Ricardo Legorreta, Fumihiko Maki, Luis Monreal, Domenico Negri and Ali Shuaibi.

Although Rasem Badran's design was endorsed by the special projects office representing the client, it was in fact the second choice of the independent jury: the members unanimously favoured Charles Correa's scheme, particularly for its contemporary and symbolic input.

While Badran's scheme was appreciated by the jury for having its roots in Muslim heritage and for providing an urban image that would reflect the city's history and uses of contemporary architectural language, they expressed some concern about the project's ability to respond to unknown future uses due to the formal rigidity of the proposal. Multiple access was also considered problematic in terms of security.

Badran's project embraces the historical culture of Doha while incorporating principles of Gulf architecture and planning; emulating organic growth in the urban landscape. The structural system is reinforced concrete frames with stone cladding. The roof plane is conceived as a fifth 'facade' in its provision of a pedestrian promenade. Gallery roofs are wood-covered steel structures supported on exterior columns. A central connecting point is provided by the plaza, which is located at the heart of the public area, adjacent to the main public entrance. The gardens in view of the galleries are integrated into the museum but can be visited independently.

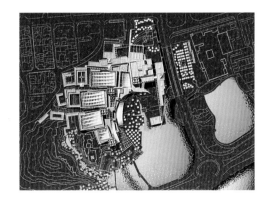
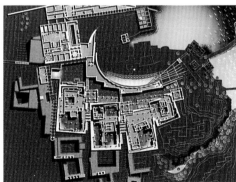

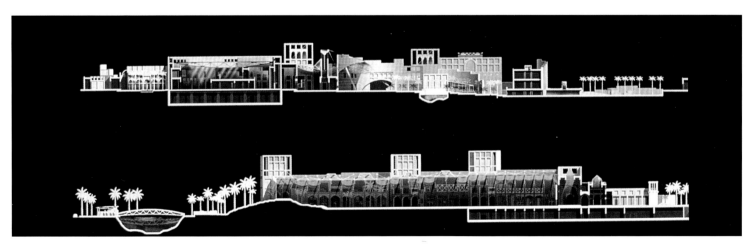

Rasem Badran's competition-winning proposal – OPPOSITE, FROM ABOVE: Computer rendering of aerial perspective; model;
FROM ABOVE, L TO R: Site plan; ground floor plan; first floor plan; sections

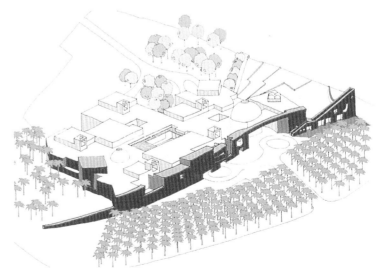

*Charles Correa's proposal – FROM ABOVE, L TO R: Model;
computer rendering of exterior; aerial perspective*

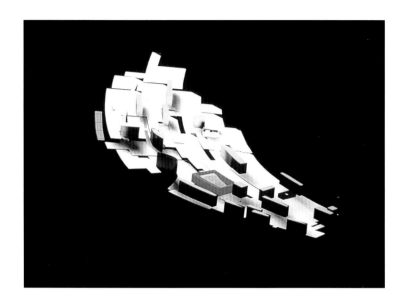
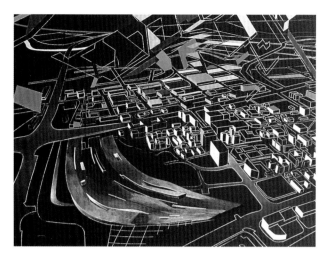
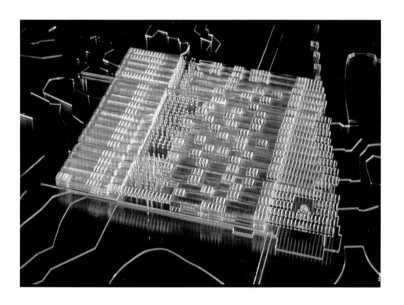

View of the window to the bay at the end Great Hall

ABOVE, L TO R: Zaha Hadid, computer model; landscape study painting of aerial view; CENTRE, L TO R: Richard Rogers, model; perspective of exterior; BELOW, L TO R: James Wines, model; drawing of aerial view

Hi Juliet

I hope you have a fantastic celebration! I'll email the ladies to remind them.

I would like to donate 4 free tickets for OFF THE CUFF at the Greenwich Picturehouse on Sunday 8th January. They will also get £5 reduced entry to future OFF THE CUFF's. Let me know the winners names and email/phone numbers and I will contact them with the details and put the tickets on the door for them.

If you could give a little anouncement on Saturday night of our Sunday gig at the Rosemary Branch (7.30pm start) that would be fantastic!

Enjoy!
xx

Ali Adolph, Short And Girlie Productions
... making your life more dramatic
www.shortandgirlie.com

Short And Girlie Productions is a not-for-profit organisation and operate on a voluntary basis.

WHERE: Screening Room, Greenwich Picturehouse, 180 Greenwich High Road, SE10 8NN
TRAVEL: Greenwich (train and DLR) / Cutty Sark (DLR)
WHEN: every 2nd Sunday of the month - from Sunday 8th January @ 7.30pm
COST: £8.50 usual price / £5 concessions or if registered on our database ?
register@shortandgirlie.com
TICKETS: 08707 550065 /
http://www.picturehouses.co.uk/site/cinemas/Greenwich/local.html

CHAIX & MOREL AND ASSOCIATES

TEPEE – GEORGES POMPIDOU CENTRE
Paris

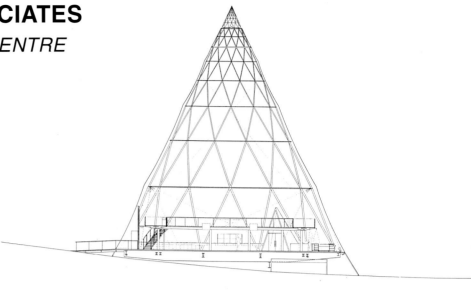

The tepee is a temporary structure that has been erected while the Pompidou Centre is provisionally closed for works. It was conceived in 1992 to provide a temporary reception area for the Toulouse Lautrec Exhibition at the Grand Palais, and was also used by the Bibliothèque de France to explain the effects of the surrounding works to the public.

In the morning, the space is reserved for group pedagogical activities. In the afternoon, it is open to everyone for information and CD-Rom or Internet access. In the evening, the space is used for meetings, shows and debates. A library also offers information on the Pompidou Centre in addition to a programme that caters for different languages.

While the impression of a large white cone is predominant externally, the tepee reveals its metallic geometry under the diffused light of the interior. Within the fabric cladding, the structural arrangement of isoceles triangles draws the eye upwards.

During the day, the tepee's fabric appears matt. The fabric of the tepee allows light to be diffused internally. At night, radiant light emphasises the transparency and structural pattern of the cone.

FROM ABOVE, L TO R: Section; structural geometry; site plan; plan

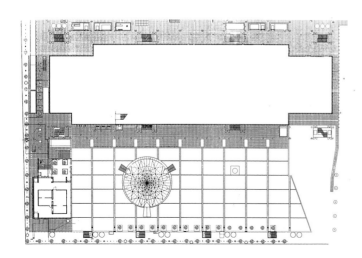

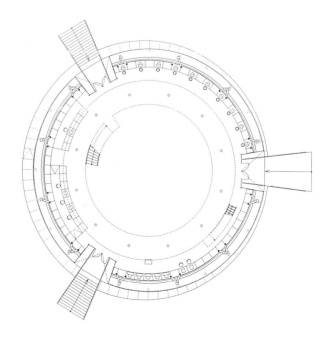

Reviews
Books

Books

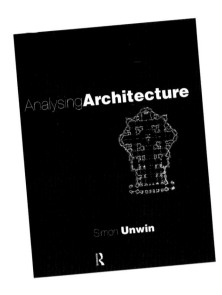

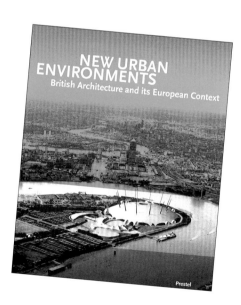

Analysing Architecture, *Simon Unwin, Routledge (London), 208pp, b/w ills, HB £50 PB £17.99*

This book is not the objective examination of architecture that the title and austerity of the cover implies. It is a collection of personal thoughts upon how the author feels we may dissect building. To its merit this kind of analysis attempts to demystify some seminal works of architecture and distils architecture to a series of simple and accessible concepts. The complex interrelationships of architectural ideas are subjected to an investigation which although serious is simply translated.

Architecture is a synthetic activity, bringing together diverse and often contradictory requirements. The book attempts to illustrate the reverse of this process by establishing a series of analytical 'filters' through which to dissect architecture. This is, of course, an ambitious project. Can one system really explain all endeavours, from the most primitive to the most contemporary?

Unwin subscribes to a particular view of theory that supposes architecture derives from a set of timeless principles of form which transcend the particularities of designers, cultures and climates. The 'conceptual' filters that Unwin employs are sometimes appropriate and predictable, including themes such as Architecture and its relationship to 'Place', as informed by Geometry, as modelled in 'Light', and acting as an 'Environmental Modifier' etc.

However, in other instances these filters seem peculiarly idiosyncratic: an inconclusive comparison of 'the Temple' and 'the Cottage', 'Elements doing more than one thing' and 'Using things that are there'! Of course, all of the latter are possible ways in which to look at architecture. However, in contrast to other methods of comparison, they present the reader with a particularly defined analytical framework.

The strong theme and method that emerges from the book is that of conceptually framing architecture in order to isolate particular issues from the complexity that is the final product. Having proposed a method, Unwin proceeds to test its voracity by application to case study, choosing five buildings: Vanna Venturi House, Fitzwilliam College Chapel, Merrist Wood, Schminke House and the Woodland Chapel.

Not surprisingly, these examples lend themselves to the analytical framework posited. The analysis of Schminke House appears particularly relevant to the author's themes and that of Merrist Wood leaves a feeling of wanting to know more.

These studies are a useful illustration of 'how to' analyse architecture in terms previously described in the book, at this point the sketches, plans and sections serve well and complement as analytical thinking drawings.

Conversely, one could consider the criteria used by Unwin difficult to apply universally: what of 'servant and served' or 'figure and ground'. Of course, one could frame and re-frame architecture according to one's own predispositions.

However, to level the critique of non-inclusivity at Unwin's book would clearly be unfair, such predispositions are inherently diverse and subject to infinitesimal subdivision. To try to suggest the terms by which one can define architecture is an unrewarding task, always subject to the criticism that one has excluded one view, or inappropriately included another. Unwin has accepted this dichotomy and opted for a more personal stance. He intersperses the book with his own drawings which serve to punctuate and enlighten the text. It may miss some of the finer points, yet goes a long way towards engaging the reader in many of the central ideas which underlie architecture. As such, one would have no hesitation in recommending this book to new students: it introduces many ideas and references central to the study of architecture. The case studies are particularly informative. A student would find this a useful aid to identifying the many important issues seriously engaged with in Architecture. *Lorraine Farrelly*

New Urban Environments: British Architecture and its European Context, *edited by Peter Murray and MaryAnne Stevens, Prestel (Munich), 192pp, colour ills, PB, £39.95*

This book catalogues the work of over 50 contemporary British architects featured in a travelling exhibition presented in association with the Japan UK Festival '98. Their work is preceded by two short commentaries by Robert Maxwell and Richard Burdett and distributed into eight sections summarising the urban context, public buildings, transport, leisure, culture, commerce and ecology.

The selection brings together large- and small-scale examples of built work and projects. Not only does it cover well-trodden ground (Paternoster Square, Waterloo, Bankside, the Millennium Dome, Bridge and Wheel, The British Library, South Bank) but it highlights a number of lesser-known schemes such as the Imperial War Museum near Manchester, the Corn Exchange in King's Lynn, the National Space Science Centre in

Reviews

Books

Leicester, the Weather-Watch Discovery Centre, Bracknell, and the Peckham Library and Media Centre in London.

The choice of buildings (many with the accent on 'high-tech') reflects the diversity that is synonymous with British design – currently enjoying a somewhat salubrious position in the field of fashion. As well as assembling the 'here and now', the book forecasts the future with a great many unbuilt schemes.

Sensous Architecture: The Art of Erotic Building, *Christian W Thomsen, Prestel (Munich), 184pp, colour ills, HB, £39.95*
This book replenishes the steady stream of discourse relating to architecture and the 'body' which emerged in the 80s, and has continued well into the 90s. Aaron Betsky's *Building Sex*, and Richard Sennett's *Flesh and Stone* are just two examples of this trend.

The new body cult of the 90s, Thomsen suggests, is connected with the apparent demise of the body that in turn is related to Modernism's tendency towards abstraction. The two main tendencies pinpointed in architecture are the dominance of the purely functional, and the apparent reduction in body mass along the lines of media architecture

In addition to Thomsen's lively coverage of such aspects as bath culture and sensuality, erotic symbols in architecture, erotic architecture fantasies, city ambience and sense appeal, and cybersex – the book includes two essays by Angela Krewani. These are informative contributions, seductively entitled 'De Sade and High Tech: Body-Architecture and Fantasies of Dismemberment', and 'Architecture and Eroticism in Film'.

Sensous architecture, it seems, is characterised by a multisensory interplay of shapes, colours, bodies and light: Hollein's Retti Candle Shop and Abteiberg Museum, the temple of Khajuraho and the 'wrapped' Reichstag are among the many examples that are considered to possess these properties. Thomsen reveals that although we are often aware of the more obvious symbolism afforded by the vertical (Lebbeus Woods' Biomechanical, Biodynamic and Proto-mechanical towers are a fine example), sometimes it is the plan that holds the key, as revealed by the phallic organisation of Stanley Tigerman's Daisy House, completed in the 1970s.

Occasionally, however, architects leave nothing to the imagination: Nicholas Schöeffer's proposals for a cybernetic city in 1959 incorporated a sexual leisure centre shaped like a woman's breast – an undeniable assertion of the physical nature of architecture, in contrast to the androgynous figure earmarked for London's 'Thrillennium' Dome. This book is to be recommended, if at least for its eyebrow-raising content. It is an extensive study that makes the most of its fleshy content with numerous colour illustrations, relieving the eyes from a rather tiny script.
Iona Spens

Architecture and Cubism, *edited and with an introduction by Eve Blau and Nancy J Troy, MIT Press (Cambridge Mass), HB, £29.95*
Books culled from conference papers often seem disjointed. Too often they comprise a series of unconnected thoughts around the conference subject forged together with little editorial input other than an introduction which tells the story of the conference in order to justify the rag bag collection that follows. I regret that *Architecture and Cubism* only goes to reinforce this view.

Many of the essays (we are not told which) were originally presented at such a conference organised by the Canadian Centre for Architecture in 1993. Reading the book is like panning for gold: you have to sift through a great deal of worthless excess in order to find the occasional nugget! My sifting revealed three of the 11 papers worthy of that effort.

Beatriz Colomina's 'Where are we?' deals with the central cubist question, of the observer's viewpoint relative to the world as experienced, while Yves-Alain Bois' short essay cuts through accepted 'cubist architecture' to reveal a deeper interpretation.

Bruno Rechlin makes some interesting comments concerning the paintings of Le Corbusier, providing an insight into the painter-architect. He quotes Corb as follows:

These paintings and drawings date to 1920 when, at the age of thirty-three, I began painting. I have been painting ever since, every day, mastering the secrets of form wherever I can find them, developing the spirit of invention just as an acrobat daily develops his muscles and self control.

In fact, if one can detect any theme through the essays it is probably that of Le Corbusier as the Picasso of architecture, although this exploration was made long ago by Colin Rowe and Robert Slutsky in their papers *Transparency: Literal and Phenomenal* of 1955-56 (not published until 1963 and 1971).

It is not surprising that many of the contributors to *Architecture and Cubism* rely as their starting point on the thoughts of Rowe and Slutsky, or Sigfried Gideon's seminal analogy

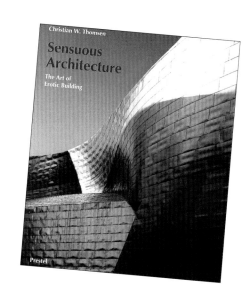

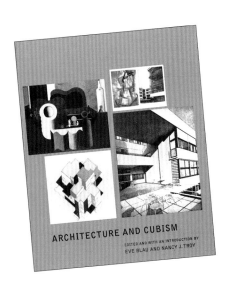

Reviews
Books

Books

(in *Space, Time and Architecture*) involving Picasso's *L'Arlesienne* and the glazed corner of Gropius' Dessau Bauhaus.

The four essays that I mentioned are grouped towards the end of the book. Anyone less than the keenest academic will probably have given up long before reaching them. The rest of the essays in *Architecture and Cubism* fall into two categories: The quirky, 'The Architecture of the Cubist Poem'; or the particular, 'The French imprint on Czech Architecture 1910-14'. They are therefore of little interest to anyone other than a specialist.

As might be expected from a collection of papers prepared by academics at a conference for academics, much of the writing falls into a kind of impenetrable 'Intellectual Speak' – the kind of language characterised by the liberal use of terms like 'historiography', 'sociopoliticised' and 'poststructural methodological', along with seemingly endless sentences and more footnotes than text. This, again, is a reflection on the book as a collection, lacking editorial direction in initially determining the audience of the publication.

Added to the wanting quality of the text is the paucity of illustrative material, all of which is monochrome! The world of the cubist painters and architects was constructed of planes of 'colour', and while Gideon's *Space, Time and Architecture* of 1941 had no choice of reproduction other than black and white, surely for a book costing £29.95 the absence of any colour plates can only be seen as pennypinching on the part of the publishers.

All of this is a great shame, for the impact that the ideas of cubism have made on the way in which man's understanding of the world changed in the 20th century is far reaching and deeply ingrained, especially in architecture. As such, this book is a missed opportunity for the serious reflection and evaluation of this impact at the end of the century.

The message for all prospective conference organisers is clear: no matter how successful the event or how illuminating the proceedings, a collection of papers does not make a book. The message for prospective readers of *Architecture and Cubism* is equally clear – it is better to go back to the original sources and read Gideon, or Rowe and Slutsky. Of the latter, perhaps the publishers might reconsider changing the uninviting title, *Transparency: Literal and Phenomenal*, to something more direct, more catchy; maybe something along the lines of 'Architecture and Cubism'? It could be a seller!   *Martin Pearce*

Sverre Fehn: Works, Projects, Writings, 1949-1996, *Christian Norberg-Schulz and Gennaro Postiglione, The Monacelli Press (New York), colour ills, HB, £50*

Once again The Monacelli Press has published a beautiful volume, intelligently compiled with important subject matter. The work of Sverre Fehn sets a standard of theory and practice revered throughout the world, although he has not quite achieved the 'superstar' status which follows many architects today. Fehn believes that, 'Architecture is basically philosophy. Man moves in it from one space to another, from one philosophical view to another'.

From his ground-breaking Norwegian Pavilion for the 1958 Brussels Exposition and his 1962 Pavilion for the Nordic Nations at the Venice Biennale, through to winning the Pritzker Prize in 1997 and beyond, Sverre Fehn has experienced a fascinating career. Faithfully retaining his Modernist principles and his own poetics, his main areas of concern centre around the division of space according to a psychological model; a continuity between exterior and interior, and between nature and architecture; the interpretation of context and an expressive representation of its elements through structure and material.

Francesco Dal Co contributes a provocative and insightful introduction to the influences on Fehn as a designer which draws the reader through the journey of his life and demonstrates his talent. Christian Norberg Schulz describes the chronological development of Fehn's work in the context of the time and analyses the oeuvre with his extreme authority and intellect.

Gennaro Postiglione's contribution is pivotal with his poetic texts and the 50 project presentations which clearly explain each scheme with sketches, drawings and photographs. In some cases the images are exquisite. Added to all this is an anthology of writings by Sverre Fehn and critics, a register of works, as well as a bibliography and biography completing this comprehensive study. The book in itself is beautiful and is an essential portrait for anyone with even the most vague interest in this Nordic architect and educator.

Maggie Toy

Erratum: *In the January/February issue of* AD *('Consuming Architecture'), OMA's competition scheme for the Luxor Theatre was miscredited as 'competition-winning' scheme. The winning scheme was, in fact, by Bolles + Wilson, whose scheme will be featured at a later date. We apologise for this error.*

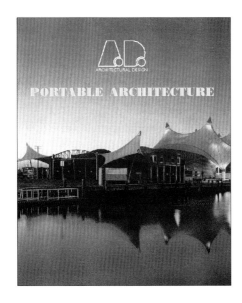

PORTABLE ARCHITECTURE

AD Profile 135

Guest-edited by Robert Kronenburg

This issue of *Architectural Design* presents a compilation of essays and projects by leading practitioners in the field of tensile and related structures. As land prices increase and building budgets are cut, there is an ever-increasing need for buildings which can be moved from one site to another. This issue features examples of residential, leisure, business and industrial portable structures that are being developed to overcome challenges which static structures cannot cope with.

Developed from an international symposium and exhibition held at the Royal Institute of British Architects, London in 1997, the book features projects by Lorenzo Apicella, Richard Horden, Buro Happold and FTL, in addition to the spectacular stage sets created by Mark Fisher – most recently known for his designs for U2, The Rolling Stones and Pink Floyd.

• Stimulating text and images
• Clear and authoritative coverage of a fascinating and topical subject

PB 0471-98422-1, 305 x 252 mm, 112 pages. Y29.95 $29.95 £18.99: September/October 1998

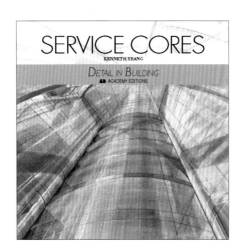

SERVICE CORES

Kenneth Yeang

DETAIL IN BUILDING

This title in the *Detail in Building* series (which has previously focused on staircases, soft canopies, glass canopies, columns) is intended to assist designers in the planning and design of service cores in high-rise buildings and to demonstrate their integral necessity in the initial plan of the structure. Utilising case studies and technical information, it is invaluable to architects, engineers and designers in countries where extensive high-rise buildings are being designed or constructed. Author of the best-selling *Skyscraper Bioclimatically Considered*, Kenneth Yeang examines the complications involved in incorporating the service core and the most suitable methods of achieving sustainable high-rise environments.

• An essential guide for architects and structural engineers
• Unusual and innovative case studies
• Part of the *Detail in Building* series

PB 0471-97904- X, 245 x 245 mm, 96 pages. Y32.50 $32.50 £18.99: May 1998

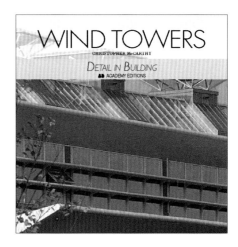

WIND TOWERS

Christopher McCarthy

DETAIL IN BUILDING

This is the first text to provide a unique step-by-step guide to the design development of wind towers. It provides case studies of modern wind towers and technical information on their construction and is intended to assist architects and engineers in the development of towers used to help reduce the energy consumption in buildings, such as shopping malls, sports stadia and offices.

The growing demand for naturally ventilated buildings to replace air-conditioned structures is epitomised in the case study of the New Parliament Building, currently under construction, designed by Michael Hopkins & Partners.

Christopher McCarthy is a partner in Battle McCarthy Consultant Engineers. He lectures at University College London and the Royal College of Art and has been a regular contributor to *Architectural Design*.

• An essential guide for architects and structural engineers
• Unusual and innovative case studies
• Part of the *Detail in Building* series

PB 0471-98087- 0, 245 x 245 mm, 96 pages. Y32.50 $32.50 £18.99: May 1998

Exhibitions

THE CAMPAIGN AGAINST LIVING MISERABLY

ROYAL COLLEGE OF ART GALLERIES

London

This exhibition in May brought together the work of 12 artists from a variety of countries. United in their attempt to make sense of the everyday environment, the artists present an alternative vision for the viewer, their expressions ranging from the surreal and enigmatic to the seemingly 'normal'.

For some artists, such as Simon Faithfull, amelioration takes the form of escape. The chosen method is *Escape Vehicle No 5*, a kitchen chair suspended from a helium balloon – the simplicity of this surreal, child-like vision is strangely reassuring.

Disturbing upon closer inspection is Miles Coolidge's documentation of Safetyville, 'a theme park of the normal or everyday'. The town, which was created to teach schoolchildren to cross the roads, displays no signs of inhabitation or flux – a Disneyland without the characters.

More straightforward and typically in tune with today's minimalist currency is the work of Atelier van Lieshout, a Dutch organisation which has collaborated previously with Rem Koolhaas. Using inexpensive materials, they create clean and practical domestic living units. One project, *Study/Book Skull*, is like a human hive. This small retreat provides a space for study/intellectual activity.

Another depiction of domestic living is presented by Tom Hunter, a self-styled community photographer. In *Tower Block*, he documents the lives of residents in a soon-to-be demolished housing estate in Holly Street, Hackney, his portraits drawing attention to the destruction of the personal environment. In lending poise and dignity to the scene these pictures challenge any preconceptions the observer may have possessed.

Our clarity of vision is shattered by the chaos of Tomoko Takashi's analytical installations. However, it seems there is method in the apparent madness – the chaos is an arrangement of the highest order, its staccato quality betraying its structured organisation. In turn, we are confronted with the privileged nature of our clutter when viewing the improvised collection of objects in *Inventory*, by Cuban artist Gabinete de Diseño Ordo Amoris and her team.

For those who lead an unsheltered life, artist Lucy Orta offers an alternative with 'Body Architecture'. Her versatile Archigram-style garb offers its inhabitant the choice of metamorphosis. With its outlets for limbs and heads, Orta's expansive tent-suit is a stylish reminder of the homeless situation.

For the more privileged lifestyle, N55 has created a Home Hydroponic Unit. This movable facility allows fruit and vegetables to be grown in the comfort of the urban home. Less mess, more flavour. Why shelve books to feed the mind when you could be shelving vegetables?

Iona Spens

Miles Coolidge, Safetyville, *1994*

Simon Faithfull, Escape Vehicle No 5, *1996*

Lucy Orta, Body Architecture, *1994*

Atelier van Lieshout, Study/Book Skull, *1996*

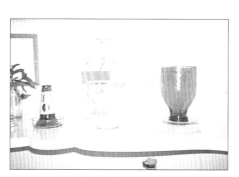

Gabinete de Diseño Ordo Amoris, Inventory, *1996; RIGHT: N55*, Home Hydroponic Unit, *1997*

Exhibitions

JAPAN 2000

ARCHITECTURE AND DESIGN FOR THE JAPANESE PUBLIC

Art Institute of Chicago

This travelling exhibition focuses on the latest trends in the fields of architecture and design to emerge in post-war Japan. It is the result of a collaboration between the Art Institute of Chicago's department of architecture and the Japan Foundation, acknowledging the ties that exist between Chicago and Japan, manifested in the work of Frank Lloyd Wright for example.

The buildings and objects featured are the product of government patronage – public works that most clearly embody the spirit of the time. Typically, and despite Japan's rich architectural tradition, many buildings erected immediately after the war were built with reinforced concrete, standardised and characterless.

While the spark of individuality could be discerned in the 50s, in works such as Togo Murano's World Peace Memorial Cathedral and Kenzo Tange's Peace Centre in Hiroshima, it was in the 60s that the situation showed a marked improvement, partly as a result of economic growth and

partly in preparation for the 1964 Tokyo Olympics. Not surprisingly, the consumer-oriented world of the 70s and 80s culminated in the uninhibited formal grammar of Post-Modernism. It was not really until the late 80s, however, that greater opportunity in the public arena was given to a younger generation of architects.

A seminal vehicle for this was ArtPolis: a series of projects sponsored by the government of Kumamoto Prefecture, advised by Arata Isozaki. This included work by Ando, Takamatsu, Hasegawa, Sejima, Yoh, Ito and Takeyama. Significantly, other prefectures were encouraged to follow suit, such as Toyama and Okayama.

Although recent economic upheavals have clearly affected the volume of new public commissions, the exhibition reflects a vigorous approach to design. Some projects evoke traditional associations, such as Kengo Kuma's Noh Stage in the Forest, Toyoma (1996), or Jun Aoki's dynamic Mamihara Bridge (1995) which

flirts with the concept of the traditional Japanese arched bridge. Others exercise more ethereal concerns: Teiichi Takahashi's 'Buoyant Cloud' Stadium in Kumamoto (1997) incorporates a pneumatic membrane, while Kisho Kurokawa's Fukui City Museum of Art (1996) is a fluid definition of lightness and transparency.

Alternatively, a more sober form of monumentality is presented by Isozaki's project for a police station in Okayama (1996) with its dense forest of steel columns; likewise, Fumihiko Maki's sculptural Kaze-no-Oka Crematorium in Natatsu (1997).

What emerges from the selected works, especially the highly sophisticated range of design products, is an obvious interest in experimentation. This is something we readily associate with Japan – a nation that is constantly in a state of flux – and with a country that is prone to wrestling with new ways to address its overcrowded situation.

Iona Spens

Masayuki Kurokawa, chaos wristwatch

Fumihiko Maki, Kaze-no-Oka Crematorium, Natatsu, 1997

Styling Division, Daihatsu Midget II, 1996

Motormi Kawakami, desk, mirror and chest of drawers, 1994

Teiichi Takahashi, 'Buoyant Cloud' Stadium, Kumamoto, 1997

The exhibition runs from 6 June until 7 September 1998. An accompanying publication, Japan 2000: Architecture and Design for the Japanese Public, edited by John Zukowsky, is published by Prestel c/o Biblios (West Sussex)

Bologna 14th - 18th October 1998

INTERNATIONAL BUILDING EXHIBITION

SAIE is one of the great international building fairs that few can afford to miss. Which is why last year no fewer than 170,000 visitors converged on Bologna from all over the world. This year SAIE is preparing to meet the requirements of its 1,900 exhibitors with 220,000 sq.m. of display space, where a comprehensive line-up of building materials and services will be arranged in sectors. Yet SAIE also stages over 50 conferences and meetings during the show, offering professionals an exceptional opportunity to examine and discuss technical, environmental and land policy issues which will continue to be closely connected to the growth of the market over the coming years.

EXHIBITORS SECTOR:
- *WATERPROOFING AND INSULATION.*
- *EXHIBITION OF TOOLS AND FASTENING SYSTEMS.*
- *BUILDING MATERIALS AND PRODUCTS.*
- *BUILDING SYSTEMS, COMPONENTS AND SUBSYSTEMS.*
- *MACHINERY AND EQUIPMENT FOR THE INDUSTRIAL PRODUCTION OF BUILDING COMPONENTS.*
- *BUILDING SITE MACHINERY, EQUIPMENT AND TECHNOLOGIES. SPECIAL MACHINERY AND EQUIPMENTS FOR CIVIL ENGINEERING WORKS.*
- *CONTROL AND MEASURING INSTRUMENTS AND EQUIPMENT FOR TESTING.*
- *PLUMBING, PIPING AND WATER TREATMENT.*
- *COMPUTERS SYSTEMS - SERVICE COMPANIES.*

SAIE 98

Fiere Internazionali di Bologna - Ente Autonomo - Viale della Fiera, 20 - 40128 Bologna - Italy
Tel. 051-282111 fax 051-282332 - E-mail: dir.com@bolognafiere.it - Internet: www.bolognafiere.it/SAIE

THE EVERYDAY AND ARCHITECTURE

REWI THOMPSON ARCHITECTS, INTERIOR OF PUUKENGA MAORI EDUCATION CENTRE, AUCKLAND, NEW ZEALAND

Architectural Design

THE EVERYDAY AND ARCHITECTURE

OPPOSITE: BEHNISCH & BEHNISCH, MAIN ADMINISTRATIVE BUILDING OF THE LANDESVERSICHERUNGSANSTALT SCHLESWIG-HOLSTEIN, LÜBECK, 1994-97
ABOVE: LE K ARCHITECTURES, ZONE B, EUROPEAN 4, 1996, SQUARE AND 'HOTEL DU LANDY'

ACADEMY EDITIONS • LONDON

Acknowledgements

We would like to express our gratitude to all the contributors to *Architectural Design* and in particular to Sarah Wigglesworth and Jeremy Till for guest-editing this issue.

Sarah Wigglesworth and Jeremy Till would like to thank all the contributors for their support and input during the compilation of this issue. In addition we would like to thank Phillip Hall-Patch for initial research; Faculty of Design, Kingston University for research support; Katharina Ledersteger-Goodfriend and Tony Roch for their translations; Rodney Hill of Jay Gorney Modern Art, New York; Carrie Jones at RoTo Architects; Christian Kandzia at Behnisch and Partner; Anna Lockyer of Rewi Thompson Ltd, Architect; Julian Maynard Smith of Station House Opera; Jackie, Margaret and Sarah Mockbee.

Photographic Credits: *p2* property of K Herman and J Sigwalt; *p6* Susana Bruell; *p12* Rob White; *p14 above left* Michael O'Brien-Thumm; *above right* Stevie Whitson, *below* Julian Maynard Smith; *p15* Julian Maynard Smith; *pp24-25* images are frame enlargements from *Robinson in Space* (Patrick Keiller, 1997, 83 min), a BBC film distributed by the British Film Institute and available as a Connoiseur/Academy Video; *p29* Gillian Horn; *p30 left* Atlas Caravan Company, *centre* ABI Leisure Homes, *right* Cosalt Holiday Homes; *p34 centre, below* David Grandorge; *p36* Annely Juda Fine Art, London ©; *p38 left* Sumita Sinha, *centre and right* Susana Bruell ©; *p39* Takanobu Sakuma; *p40 below left, p41 below right* Stephen Piotrowski; *pp42-47* Níall McLaughlin; *p48* Richard Glover; *p49 above* Julie Phipps, *below* Ben Kelly; *p50, p51* Richard Davies ©; *pp52-56* Jamie Parslow; *pp58-61* Darcy Hemley; *pp66-71* RoTo Architects Inc; *p72, pp74-77* Timothy Hursley, The Arkansas Office; *p73, pp78-79* Samuel Mockbee; *pp80-83, pp84-87* images property of K Herman and J Sigwalt; *pp88-95* Christian Kandzia, Behnisch and Partner.

Front Cover: Samuel Mockbee, The Harris House, Greensboro, Alabama
Inside Covers: Níall McLaughlin, Shack, Foxhall, Northamptonshire, computer-generated image

EDITOR: Maggie Toy
DEPUTY EDITOR: Ellie Duffy
DESIGN: Mario Bettella and Andrea Bettella/Artmedia

First published in Great Britain in 1998 by *Architectural Design*
42 LEINSTER GARDENS, LONDON W2 3AN

A division of John Wiley & Sons
Baffins Lane, Chichester, West Sussex PO19 1UD

ISBN: 0-471-98424-8

The Publishers and Editor do not hold themselves responsible for the opinions expressed by the writers of articles or letters in this magazine
Copyright of articles and illustrations may belong to individual writers or artists
Architectural Design Profile 134 is published as part of
Architectural Design Vol 68 7-8/1998
Architectural Design Magazine is published six times a year and is available by subscription

Printed and bound in Italy

Contents

ARCHITECTURAL DESIGN PROFILE No 134
THE EVERYDAY AND ARCHITECTURE
Guest-edited by Sarah Wigglesworth and Jeremy Till

Elemer Zalotay, House in Ziegelried, Switzerland

SARAH WIGGLESWORTH AND JEREMY TILL
THE EVERYDAY AND ARCHITECTURE

You are reading these words, but first you have taken the smooth covers of the magazine in your hands, flicked them, released the dense aroma of printing ink, stopped at an image suffused with colour, moved to another imbued with lusciousness and now you are thinking: 'How can this be The Everyday?' Now look up, wriggle your toes, sense the presence of others who have occupied, are occupying or will occupy the space you are in. Focus: find those cracks through which time, dirt, fear, passion, event have entered to disturb the idealised, static, perfection of that space's conception. Now shut the magazine and turn it over. Hold that shiny cover in front of your face and worry whether that white mark is a speck of dirt on the surface or a spot on your face. Relieve that worry by bending the cover, distorting the space beyond and your image occupying it.

This issue of *Architectural Design* attempts to capture the fragility of that distorted reflection, where image and reality blur. It accepts that the everyday will rush in to disturb the impossible vanity and perfection of architecture, but sees this action as ultimately productive. Our tactic is not that of the hair-shirt puritan; we aim to seduce you with the gloss, and slip the world of the everyday in through the back door.

We first came to the everyday from the furthest shores of architecture. Conceived of as an island, this architecture concerns itself with internalised notions of form and style. Aesthetics and technology enter into an unholy alliance which allows the self-contained and self-referential languages of architecture continually to evolve. Occasionally boats arrive at this island, bringing with them fresh supplies of theory, geometry and technique which inject the flagging body of architecture with new life. It is not surprising that the architecture which is thereby created is obsessed with notions of the iconic, the one-off, the monumental. It privileges the final product over the process, the perfected moment of completion over the imperfections of occupation. It concerns itself with lofty ideals rather than gritty realism, searching for the next novelty whilst forgetting the present.

But of course we didn't really come to the everyday from the furthest shores of architecture. The everyday was always there, and we, like everyone else, were always immersed in it. To some extent it is this immersion which prevents us from seeing the everyday, or acknowledging it. But it is also from this immersion that specialised disciplines, among them architecture, attempt to escape. These disciplines require a distance from the ordinary in order to define themselves as something set apart and (crucially) thereby place themselves in a position to exert control and power. In this the profession of architecture is no different from any other profession. However, where it does differ is that its products, among them buildings, are inevitably involved in the vicissitudes of the everyday world. The problem arises when the actions of this world confront the isolated value system under which architecture is normally conceived – when repetitive

practices occupy the one-off, when the humble street contains the monumental, when the minor event interrupts the grand narrative – when the kid with muddy boots drags herself across the pristine spaces of iconic modernism. Here the conceit is revealed. There is something inexorable about quotidian actions which architecture is helpless to resist. Any discipline which denies the everyday will be denied everyday, and for this reason high architecture is unravelled by the habitual and banal events which mark the passage of time. There is a thudding disappointment as a gap opens up between the image of architecture and the reality of its making and occupation.

Our aim in compiling this issue is to recognise what high architecture has previously suppressed (but was never able to exclude) by seeing the world from within rather than from above. We explicitly acknowledge the everyday as a productive context for the making, occupation and criticism of architecture. However, nowhere do we attempt to define the everyday. The word alone does enough, allowing anyone to find their own space within the generalised term. Henri Lefebvre, the great philosopher of the everyday (and from whom much of our thinking develops), identifies the everyday as the residue left over when all the specialised activities have been removed. However, for us even this generalised definition sets up too oppositional a stance between the everyday and architecture (as a specialised activity). Whilst we may have introduced the everyday in distinction to high architecture, it is not our intention to get caught within the binary trap of remaining immersed in the ordinary. This would lead to the disavowal of architectural knowledge and creativity alike – knowledge because it is associated with the repressive structures of power and expertise, creativity because it is associated with uncritical genius. But this unequivocal disavowal leads to a disempowerment of user and architect alike. Instead, we suggest that the real productive potential for architects lies in an endless movement between engagement and retreat. Engagement as social beings (eating, farting, fucking), as users of spaces (and no different to the many other users of spaces), as political beings (where the personal is, as she says, political). Retreat to find an unburdened space in which to understand, to dream, to speculate. In this restless movement traditional oppositions of ideal/real, extraordinary/ordinary, universal/particular, special/everyday and so on, can never settle into a hierarchical order. Instead each member of the pair continually interprets and reformulates the other. Aspects of the world overlooked or suppressed by high architecture are thus allowed to flourish in a manner which captures the redemptive and creative potential of any act of making.

If we do not define the everyday, neither do we intend to propose an alternative aesthetic based on it. As soon as one reifies the everyday, it dissolves under the pressure of suddenly being special. The determinist turning of concept into form brings with it all the dangers of commodification and aestheticisation

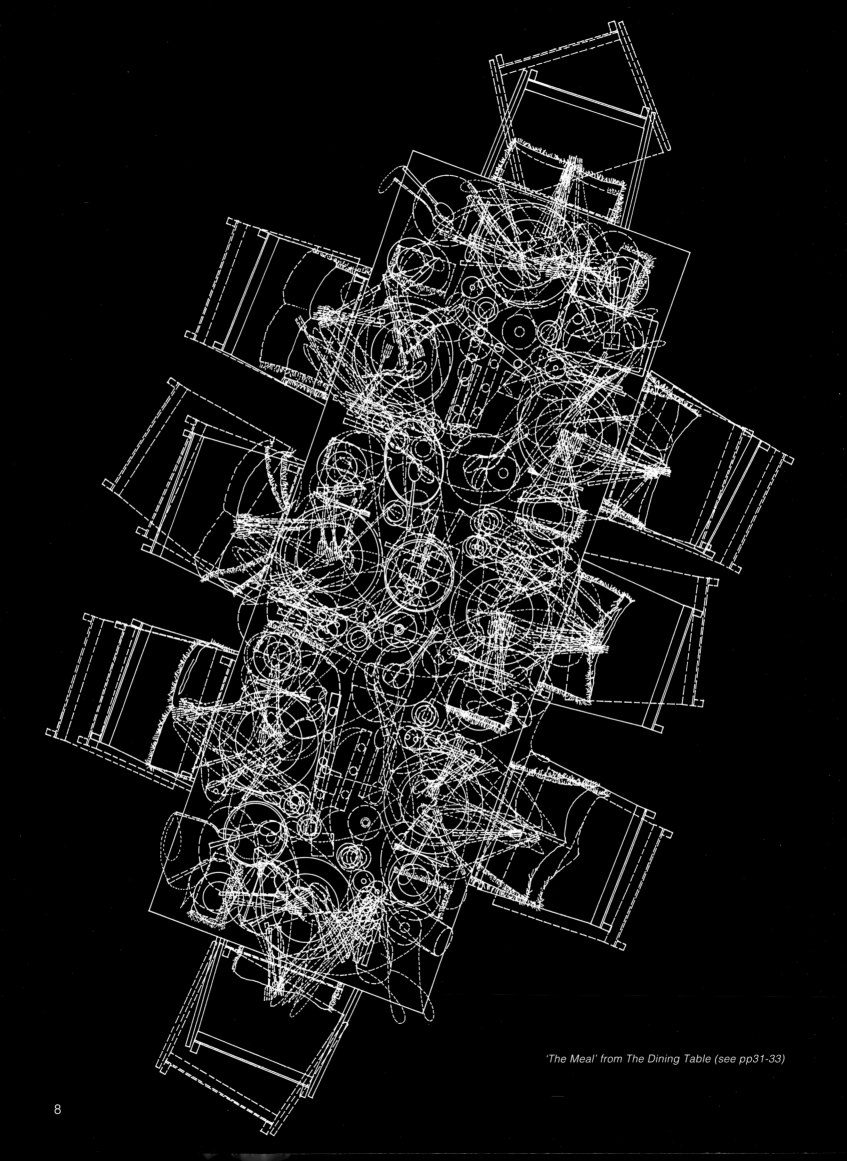

'The Meal' from The Dining Table (see pp31-33)

– a danger that we run the risk of in presenting this work within these luscious, flickable pages. However, it was never our intent to make the everyday an object of aesthetic focus. There is in this issue much more attention to the production and perception of the projects than there is to the product *per se*. It is for this reason that we did not call the issue *Architecture of the Everyday* – because that would subsume the term into the canon of architecture and suggest that architecture can represent the everyday in a reified manner. The title *The Everyday and Architecture* is meant to provide a broader context in which to place the discussion and production of architecture. Taken together, we hope that these contributions form a new awareness about how architecture may be perceived, received and made.

In compiling the issue, we found as much stimulus outside the traditional architectural field as inside. One of the obvious characteristics of the everyday is that it does not adhere to fixed classifications – it is by its very nature interdisciplinary, dissolving barriers as it passes through. Seen in a quotidian light, away from formal categories, the work of artists, writers, performers, furniture designers, and so on is absolutely relevant to architectural production. It is for this reason that we have included such work in the issue. We invited all the architects in the issue to relate their work to the general theme; the result is a critical exegesis of the process of arriving at the work rather than mere description. Led by the everyday, the compilation ranges across disciplines and melds theory with practice; for us this is a touchstone of what constitutes architectural production.

The issue is notionally divided into three sections, though these are not meant as fixed categorisations. The first section, *The (Extra)Ordinary*, deals with what is there already – the overlooked, the familiar – as opposed to what *may* be there in some kind of utopian idyll. In conventional architectural discourse these territories are overlooked precisely because they challenge the paradigms that discourse is founded upon: breeze blocks, urban backlands, dilapidated dwellings, caravans, dining tables – none of these normally appeal at an intellectual or aesthetic level. Yet these, and other, spaces of the familiar are there to be claimed and transformed into settings of extraordinary potential.

The same is true of the domestic, the place which accrues habits, disorder, stains and (traditionally) the 'volatile' lives of women and children. The domestic as a reality is an affront to normative architectural orders. So, in canonic architecture, the domestic is squeezed of any life; it is framed, ordered, set behind glass for male inspection, contorted into formal games, technicised. However, any image of control thereby created is illusory; the contingent forces of the domestic everyday are too powerful to be so suppressed. A tragic illustration of this was provided in Martin Parr's recent television series, *Signs of the Times*, which portrayed domestic interiors together with their creators. In one episode an architect describes himself as being 'under siege' as the children introduce 'rogue elements' (ie toys) into *his* interior; on the sidelines his wife privately admits her anguish at being forbidden to hang curtains. In this issue, we have encouraged such rogue elements and evidence of domestic commonplaces appear throughout.

The second section, *Making the Everyday*, brings together projects which extend the material language of architecture. It is absolutely not our intention to present the work as a fresh kind of look or as another product to be appropriated as an aesthetic. There is a tendency of some architects and artists to seize upon the contemporary world of everyday objects and turn it into a new style. Such a superficial celebration acts as a mask which deflects critical attention from the underlying forces which have shaped the production of those objects. In contrast the projects presented here do not champion the aesthetic as the end in itself, but the way that things look evolves as a result of various processes and materials of making. If there is a common language, it is one that raids the catalogues and cultural repositories outside the incredibly limited palette of conventional architecture. The fourfold appearance of straw bales is indicative of this – a happy coincidence of connections which emerged during final editing.

The final section, *Using the Everyday*, looks at how the occupation of architecture, both potential and actual, affects its production. Here the word production is used in the widest sense to incorporate the way that users themselves are producers of space. Many of the projects in this final section are for people who because of their class, race, or economic status are seen on the margins of dominant society. With all their political connotations, these margins have never been sufficiently accommodated by the values of mainstream architecture – values which too often hide behind an aesthetic mask of supposed objectivity and neutrality. In contrast, an acknowledgement of the everyday, with its engaged actions and occupations, inevitably leads to a recognition of the political and social content of architectural production. The projects in the final section suggest that in order to address these overlooked aspects, new methods of working need to be employed. They replace a prescriptive methodology or overarching strategy, with a diverse set of tactics of resistance and empowerment.

The issue opens with an elegiac piece by Greil Marcus, which could serve as an introduction to the issue as a whole. One response to reading Marcus' description of his home street is to think: 'Hey, it would be great to visit Panoramic Way next time we are in San Francisco.' That would be to miss the point altogether, because the world that Marcus (and the other contributors) opens up can be found in your street as well.

Bibliographical Note

The themes touched upon above are more fully developed in some of our other writings, most specifically: Jeremy Till, 'Angels with Dirty Faces', *Scroope*, University of Cambridge (Cambridge), 1995, vol 7, pp13-17; Jeremy Till, 'Architecture in Space, Time', in Clare Melhuish (ed), *Architecture and Anthropology*, *Architectural Design*, Academy Editions (London), vol 124, November 1996; Sarah Wigglesworth, 'Domesti-city: Reflections on Commonplaces', *Proceedings of ACSA Dallas Conference*, ACSA Publications (Washington) 1996; Sarah Wigglesworth, 'Maison de Verre: Sections through an in-vitro conception', *Journal of Architecture*, E & N Spon (London), forthcoming.

These articles also refer to two guiding authors: Henri Lefebvre, *Critique of Everyday Life*, Verso (London and New York), 1991 and *Everyday Life in the Modern World*, Transaction (New Brunswick and London), 1994 and Michel de Certeau *The Practice of Everyday Life*, University of California (Berkeley, Los Angeles and London), 1984.

GREIL MARCUS
UPWARDS DRIFT

On the level of publicity, everyday architecture in California is about utopia and commuting. I'm speaking of houses – if you cross the state, taking in the single layer birthday-cake style of the 1950s elementary and high schools, the shopping malls, airports and the like, the feeling is a lot closer to nature than that of the critical will being worked upon the environment. This stuff seems to have just happened. Nobody knows why, nobody knows how, nobody even knows when. But where people live is suffused with mysticism.

'If you lived here, you'd be home by now.' That's the great slogan of the developer trolling for home buyers as they zip on down the freeway, a good 10, 20, 30 minutes ahead of them as they pass the beckoning billboard; the weirdness of the slogan, its suggestion that, really, if you lived here you'd never have to leave at all, that somehow the world would come to you, goes into the brain like a germ. There's also the hint of the never-ending climb up the ladder of success, which also points towards an infinite regression. If you lived there, you'd be home by then, but if you lived *there*, just back down the road a few miles, you'd already be asleep. Uttered with wonder by a disembodied radio voice on the Firesign Theater's 1969 masterpiece of surrealist comedy, *How Can You Be in Two Places at Once When You're Not Anywhere At All*, or spoken into an ether of confusion by an apparently terrified David Thomas on his album *Meadville* in 1997, the slogan cannot be factored. It's unstable. Say it more than three times in a row – Thomas says it many more times than that – and the word 'home' ceases to have any meaning at all. It no longer exists.

The utopian is all over California, and less in such ridiculous piles as William Randolph Hearst's San Simeon (built by the great Bay area architect Julia Morgan, who'd do whatever you asked – you want vulgar, she'd do vulgar) than in the promethean failures of the likes of Richard Neutra and Rudolph Schindler. Neutra's gorgeous, explosively deco houses were famously unlivable (people moved in and out of the Lovell House when it wasn't empty; Hearst was happy at San Simeon); Schindler's 1921 Los Angeles prototype caused wars. Schindler, his wife Pauline and their friends Clyde and Marion Chase were bohemian perfectionists, abjuring meat in their diets and buttons on their clothes (too confining); Schindler built the four of them a house meant to assure harmony between the four humans and between humanity and nature. There was one wing, with separate sections inside, for the Schindlers, and the same for the Chases; the wings met at a communal living room and kitchen. The walls were open to the environment, with sliding glass doors instead of wood or masonry. 'Bedrooms' were sleeping areas on the flat roof of the single-storey expanse – because, as everyone knew, especially Austrians like Schindler or easterners like the other three, it never rained in California, and it was never cold.

Soon enough, the Chases moved out in rancour. The Neutras moved in. When they left, Pauline decamped to the second wing.

A schedule was set up so that she and Schindler would never have to encounter each other in the putatively shared areas of the house. They communicated only through the mail, which in those days was delivered twice a day. You could write an angry letter to your spouse in the morning and it would be delivered in the afternoon. In the 1950s, Joseph Eichler took up Schindler's basic design, and built scores of flat, glassed homes on the San Francisco Peninsula; an echo of an archaic wish to live without separation was still present.

*   *   *

Almost every day for the last 15 years, I've walked up the same steep street in the Berkeley hills, and part of what's interesting about the street, visited everyday, is that there is no hint of the commute or the utopian anywhere on it – the utopian, that is, as a quintessentially modernist, authoritarian project, with the house as a machine for living, and the people in it the fuel. The street is familiar in the way that you don't have to see it at all; it doesn't change. And in the same way you can, if you look, see something new on it every day.

The street is Panoramic Way, which changes its name to Dwight Way as it heads straight up the hill and Panoramic switchbacks hard to the left; at the top you turn left onto Panoramic again. The street begins just above the football stadium of the University of California; within one turn, if there's no noise from a game or concert to shut out, the existence of the huge arena vanishes from memory. You're on a twisting, woodsy, decaying back road in a town with no name.

Berkeley is dotted with the legacy of great architects: Morgan, Bernard Maybeck, John Galen Howard. None of them did their work on this street. The houses, most of which went up between the 1920s and the 1950s, tend to the small, the modest and the odd – the last house built on the street was started ten years ago and completed two years ago; it's big, functional, painted a dull salmon, and completely nondescript. There are two with private tennis courts, hidden from view. On the steeper parts of the street, looking up or down, you see only garages, the houses being set up or down the street level. Nothing gleams. Some years ago, Berkeley shifted from garbage haulers who'd pick up your cans wherever you kept them, to an automated system of special cans and special trucks with fork lifts – all the garbage men do is wheel the cans onto the blades. The truck dumps the contents and deposits the can back on the street. You're supposed to move your cans onto the sidewalk on your given day, then remove them, stow them out of sight. On Panoramic everyone leaves their cans out in front of their houses on a permanent basis; garbage spills out, or racoons and opossums dig in and scatter litter and rot across the yards and pavement, creating a universal feeling of slovenly collapse. The old houses on the street, especially those covered in mossy brown shingles, have a permanent cast of disrepair.

Crumbling concrete staircases, some with grand entryways and pillars, others with sweeping landings, wind up and down the hill, here and there patched and seamed, more often shot through with weeds and vines and buckling from tree roots. Pot holes open up on the road with every rain. Pine, spruce and eucalyptus, shrubs, grass, flowers and weeds seem to grow with equal rights. A sense of slow, pleasant ruin makes the street feel like its own time warp. Deer are common, along with squirrels and songbirds, floating hawks and schools of quail, an occasional coyote or rattlesnake. Warnings for mountain lions are posted, but I have never seen one. In the spring and summer you could sleep in the overgrowth on a vacant lot and live off the land, off the loquat trees, the countless varieties of plum tree; mostly out of sight, as if hiding from the fire prevention crews, are warrens of blackberry patches.

The most unsettling thing about the street is that it barely seems to be inhabited. There was a shooting here, right out in public, in plain sight, a couple of years ago; normally no one is seen out of doors. Cars run up and down, but not that often. Walking up and down for 30 minutes every day, I sometimes imagine that I am as present on this landscape as anyone who actually lives here, since it often seems as if nobody does. Peer into windows, and you see not people moving about but clutter, piles of books and papers and dishes, clutter that often looks as if it was left behind by a long-gone occupant. There's no sense that the street is more or less old or young, racially or ethnically mixed or homogeneous, filled with families or solitaries. Thus the street transcends whoever does actually live on it; it takes on a life, and a personality, of its own.

It becomes a perfect field for drifting, for what the Paris situationists of the 1950s named the *dérive*. They tried to make a playful science out of the traditions of the *flâneur* and the surrealist stroll; they once proposed a *dérive* within a single apartment. In one of the few published accounts of a full *dérive*, the reader found herself stuck in a bar. The point was to encounter the unknown as a facet of the known, astonishment on the terrain of boredom, innocence in the face of experience. So you can walk up the street without thinking, letting your mind drift, letting your legs, with their internal memory, carry you up and down and around turns, attending to a map of your own thoughts, the physical town replaced by an imaginary city. I've written more than one book doing just that. Lines come out of the air; as you turn them over in your mind, a hawk drifting on warm air currents 200 feet over your head can seem to seal any phase.

You focus your eyes on the terrain in front of you, leave your thoughts, and the very landscape seems to belong to you.

The architecture that allows the everyday to claim the terrain is an architecture that does not intrude, that is not proud – the architecture commissioned by people who want to fade in, not stand out. When a huge fire devastated large parts of Berkeley and Oakland in 1991, burning thousands of houses down to nothing, rebuilding began immediately: towers, palaces, pyramids, sultan's tombs for the living, people building onto their neighbour's land, nobody giving a flying fuck or a tinker's damn for anything but the loudest shout they could make; 'I survived! I'm a winner! Look at me!'. The new neighbourhoods that resulted are blighted with money and ego, and no sense of the everyday is possible – there is no room for accident, chance, happenstance. Intention and will are everything. But Panoramic hardly seems to have been built on at all. It's more that, for reasons no one can remember, people once found themselves here, and so built houses to keep out the rain. They died, other people moved in.

With this naturalism all around you as you climb up the hill, it can be a shock to see that, once, people did even quietly, even anonymously, find it necessary to announce their presence. Just around the first turn up the street, a brick staircase turns up towards a house you don't see, that you have to crane your neck to distinguish from the wild growth around it; it's a feature that defies you to notice anything. Yet there is a small landing after the first few steps, at the back of the landing, a small wall, and on the wall a circle, which if you look reveals itself to be a face. It's a Gorgon's mask, all curls and harsh eyes and nose sculpted out of concrete, maybe 70, maybe a 100 years ago – and the face is also a fountain. From the pipes of the house, from a hidden stream, from a pond higher up, from some source, water drips steadily out of the mouth of the face and into a dank, scummy pool of green water. Over the years as the water has dripped down the concrete below the face, an ever-widening colony of algae has taken root. The face has grown a beautiful, thick, heroic green beard, and whoever planned this is, I like to imagine, buried right beneath the little wall, watching to see if anyone notices, if anyone cares, if anyone laughs as the face is laughing. Probably, in some manner, every house on the street has a feature as distinctive, but given that the street in its ease abstracts you from it, delivering you up to the empty mansions of your own thoughts, it could take more than a life-time to stumble upon them, for in the architecture of the everyday that is just the point: not to look.

NICHOLAS TILL

THE USES OF GRAVITY

The Everyday Sublime in the Work of Station House Opera

The images are quite literally breathtaking. Projected in a darkened room they invariably elicit an exhalation of 'WOW' from an audience. In *Bastille Dances*, 8,000 breeze blocks form and reform in seemingly infinite configurations. Out of a pile of masonry resembling the ruins of an Aztec temple emerge arches and columns which then dissolve into a flow of knobbly lava. In another image human figures are suspended 50 feet in the air, ascending hopefully or toppling precipitously like the just and damned in Tintoretto's *Last Judgement*. In *Cuckoo*, bedsit cosmonauts struggle to establish precarious normality in a world in which tables, chairs and wardrobes have been unleashed from the constraints of gravity.

But the images, sublime though they may be, are only part of the story. For what we are looking at in the *Bastille Dances* sequence is not a parade of deconstructionist architectural follies. The photographs document moments of a performance event. The apparent effortlessness of the images deceive; what is frozen in the photographic picture was never permanent. As Julian Maynard Smith, the artistic director of Station House Opera, points out, 'the beautiful image is in fact not at all stable'.[1] Those blocks were lugged into place as part of a process and they only remain in place for as long as the ever shifting play of forces allows. Neither shelter nor monument, architectural form no longer strives to express meaning or function but is contingent upon human action. The flying circus in *Drunken Madness* is held in equilibrium by a precarious balance of weights and counter weights, animate and inanimate. Gravity is not here defied to provide an illusion of acrobatic weightlessness; it has become the motor of restlessness and anxiety. Repose, we are reminded, is no more than the temporary stabilisation of mighty tectonic forces.

Station House Opera operates where visual art, theatre and sculpture intersect: *Drunken Madness*, for example, is a comic Calder mobile. But Station House Opera could also be said to dramatise – meaning literally that it performs or acts out – architectural discourses of the creation of tension through dynamic equipoise. Indeed, Julian Maynard Smith initially trained as an architect, and his work consistently explores the further terrain shared by both theatre and architecture in the encounter between the human body and constructed spaces, rehearsing Bernard Tschumi's architecture of 'the interaction of space and events'.[2] Rejecting the fictional other of literary theatre, Maynard Smith explores the physical reality of that encounter between body, space and event. He seeks, as he puts it, 'to make theatre out of the physical limitations of the form'.[3] Inside the constraints of time, space and gravity Maynard Smith rediscovers something essential about theatre itself.

In *The Production of Space* Henri Lefebvre suggests that we should give 'logical and epistemological precedence over highly articulated languages with strict rules to those activities which mark the earth leaving traces and organising gestures, and work as performed in common.'[4] This is, perhaps, the essential object of theatrical representation. For the real medium of theatre is not language but human presence, and before even human presence, dramatic theorist Michael Issacharoff reminds us, is the space of performance:

> If, following Beckett's example, one can banish from a play various elements, such as movement, or even dialogue, the element that must remain constant and be retained in any text written for theatrical performance is, of course, space.[5]

Space, and the body in space, supply the dramatist's primary text, as the late Heiner Müller attested: 'The first thing that comes into my head is a feeling for space, and the configurations of people in this space. From there, gradually, a dialogue or text emerges.'[6] Theatre space defines the existence of those who inhabit it; it serves as a metaphor for individual consciousness, for social relations or for the imagined cosmos. The characters of Beckett and Müller strive for words to articulate their physical predicaments; those of earlier dramatists use socialised language to defer and conceal. Ingmar Bergmann once described Ibsen as above all a great architect, his dramas arising from the fatal dance of people struggling to demarcate terrains of private control amidst spaces threatened with public invasion.

This revised ontology of the theatrical event reveals more clearly the overlap between theatre and those architectural discourses which

Drunken Madness, *London, 1981*

have reformulated architecture's own relationship to the human body. At the Bauhaus architects and designers such as Gropius, Schlemmer and Moholy-Nagy used theatre as a means of exploring this relationship between the body and its environment, and Tschumi points to a long list of architects, from Bernini to Albert Speer, who have employed theatrical spectacle to dramatise the interaction of architectural space and human event.[7]

In such company the connotations of spectacle raise fastidious hackles. Station House Opera is well aware of this. The reference to opera in its name is an ironic, perhaps preemptive, gesture towards a spectacular art form which teeters uncertainly between sublimity and kitsch. But where baroque masque and fascist spectacle, or indeed the Wagnerian *Gesamtkunstwerk*, subordinate the human performer to the total machine (are not industrial production and the modern bureaucratic state rehearsed respectively in baroque and fascist spectacle?), Station House Opera foregrounds the efforts of the fallible human agents who engineer the show. The work thereby eschews the illusion that is so essential to conventional theatrical spectacle, revealing rather than concealing the mechanics of display. Just as there is no fictional time before or time after a Station House performance, so there is no offstage. The denizens of the Station House world operate their own elementary environments – often clumsily. There are no hidden scene shifters or rope pullers; nowhere for the *deus ex machina* to descend from. The stage manager or the puppeteer are familiar literary tropes as substitutes for God. But lacking an outside, the world of Station House Opera is resolutely unmetaphysical, confining human aspiration to the exigencies of everyday possibility. The attainment of beauty is more fragile and thereby all the more touching.

Within these exacting environments the work of Station House Opera exemplifies important phenomenological perceptions concerning the relationship of human consciousness to the material world. As Sartre suggested, 'Far from the body being first for us and revealing things to us it is the instrumental-things which in their original appearance indicate our body to us.'[8] In *Bastille Dances* the breeze blocks form an environment which dictates the being of the performers who inhabit it. The blocks create a site which Maynard Smith describes as a 'physical given . . . It's where you locate your body in relation to how you manipulate it. And how it manipulates you, as a physical thing.'[9] The performers know no other world than that which consists of blocks and they act accordingly, making and remaking their environment with dogged persistence. But however spectacular

the transformations of their world, its physical attributes remain unalterable.

Sartre also reminds us of the frailty and vulnerability of the body's relationship to the material world: 'I live my body in danger as regards menacing machines as well as manageable instruments.'[10] As Anthony Vidler has suggested, this marks a clear departure from the Renaissance paradigm of the relationship between the human body and the constructed environment founded upon the harmonious proportions of both body and world.[11] The 20th-century fragmentation of bodily self-presence leads to a more precarious relationship of man to environment. The physical world is now more hostile, so that, in Tschumi's words, 'The materiality of my body both coincides with and struggles with the materiality of space.'[12] The outcome has been an architecture which, in the manifestos of Tschumi or Coop Himmelbau, stages the struggle as a theatre of cruelty: 'We want . . . an architecture that bleeds, that exhausts, that whirls and even breaks.'[13]

This struggle between body and environment has also driven the work of phenomenological theatre makers such as the American writer/director Richard Foreman. Foreman, who believes that the fundamentals of human consciousness are 'the elementary noticings of collision between the self and its environment',[14] constructs physical worlds of fiendish complexity in which his characters have to execute apparently everyday, but actually bafflingly arbitrary, actions. A Station House Opera piece is no less rule-prescribed: the performers always have tasks to carry out, although the object of the task may be obscure. But the physical worlds in which they operate are more unstable, even more dangerous, than those which Foreman devises. Maynard Smith and his companions find themselves in Tschumi's world of 'disturbing architectural tortures'[15] in which the physical rules may have changed, but in which many of the routines and rituals of everyday life continue. There is no time for introspection, contemplation or even small talk in this environment. The reinvented physical world makes too many demands upon the performer's attention; social niceties are gratuitous in a world in which the very act of lifting a cup from a table may make the table itself, unburdened of its additional weight, shoot upwards causing the protagonist to plummet in the other direction. Survival entails a persistent repetition of everyday tasks and actions in a vain attempt to impose order on a recalcitrant world. Dramatic tension arises from the dislocations which occur when the overall formal structure is undermined by inevitable slippages.

These encounters of the everyday with a physical world more Einsteinian than Newtonian

Scenes from a New Jericho, *London, 1984*

reveal the unnoticed feats of co-ordination we each of us practise daily, from the moment we rise from our beds. We learn to ignore the virtuosity of our everyday negotiations of the physical world: the careful judgement of intention and mechanics in lifting a cup to our lips; the subtle balance of forces which sitting in a chair entails; the elegant choreography of walking along a crowded pavement. Only when the cup is too hot, or the position of the chair or the oncomer's intentions are misjudged, are we reminded how fragile our complacent mastery really is.

There is both pathos and comedy in the efforts of the Stationhousers to master and impose normalcy on their refractory world. But through that pathos and comedy we are given a glimpse into extraordinariness of the ordinary and everyday. Henri Lefebvre recognised a similarly revelatory encounter with the everyday in the work of Charlie Chaplin.

> The secret of his comic powers lies not in his body, but in the relation of this body to something else: a social relation with the material world . . . a primitive and wonderfully gifted barbarian, suddenly plunged (as we all are at every moment) into an everyday life that is inflexible and bristling with ever new difficulties . . . Suddenly he disorientates us, but only to show us what we are when faced with objects; and these objects become suddenly alien, the familiar is no longer familiar.[16]

Through this process of defamiliarisation we are led to re-examine our relationship to a material world which has become over-familiar, or alienated as commodity and sign. The imaginative re-baptism of the object restores the productive potential of our encounters with the everyday. Maynard Smith rejects the theatrical subsumption of objects as signs conveying meaning within a narrative or message and instead allows the object to speak for itself. Removed from its familiar context the physical attributes of the object – its weight, density, contours – are sharpened:

We would take something that already existed in the world, but which nobody really knows how to look at, and put it into a different context, in a sense making it visible by translating it into a different form.[17]

The formal envelopes of time, space or gravity may indeed be different. But the object retains its integrity notwithstanding. 'In the breeze block pieces, you would accept the breeze blocks – accept their physical nature, not pretending they're something else.'[18] Breeze blocks are used for construction, so in *Bastille Dances* they construct. For Station House Opera 'making strange' is not a surrealist indulgence in the metamorphosis of objects but a reaffirmation of their physical and social functions. 'The table remains a table even when its 100 feet off the ground. It's still a table.'[19]

In this re-engagement with the everyday Station House Opera effects a crucial mediation between the human and the architectural, the individual and the monumental. We do not encounter the constructed world as unsocialised beings in a series of unsocialised spaces. Mostly our negotiations of the environment are conducted through the medium of everyday objects and tasks. Maynard Smith professes no interest in those kinds of site-specific theatre which explore an architectural performance space as a given. In the work of Station House Opera the interaction of performers and their space is always negotiable, and from that negotiation of the material world there arises a primitive sociability. Lefebvre reminds us of Marx's observation that objects serve not only as goods but as a medium of social interaction, marking 'the existence of man for other men, his human relation to other men, the social behaviour of man to man.'[20] In the work of Station House Opera, the everyday object is not redeemed for its own sake, restored to a pre-lapsarian integrity which it could never have possessed. Instead, it regains its function as an agent of human sociability, forged in the space between the sublimity of aspiration and the comedy of fallibility.

Notes

1 Nick Kaye, Interview with Julian Maynard Smith, *Art into Theatre*, Harwood Academic Publishers (Amsterdam), 1996, p195.

2 Bernard Tschumi, *Architecture and Disjunction*, MIT Press (Cambridge, Mass/London), 1996, p117.

3 Kaye, op cit, p202.

4 Henri Lefebvre, *The Production of Space*, Blackwell (Oxford), 1991, p17.

5 Michael Issacharoff, 'Space and Reference in Drama', *Poetics Today*, vol 2, no 3, 1981, p211.

6 Heiner Müller, *Theatremachine*, Marc von Henning (trans), Faber & Faber (London), 1995, pxix.

7 Tschumi, op cit, p125.

8 Quoted in Anthony Vidler, *The Architectural Uncanny*, MIT Press (Cambridge, Mass/London), 1992, p81.

9 Kaye, op cit, p201.

10 Quoted in Vidler, op cit, p81.

11 Ibid, p73.

12 Tschumi, op cit, p39.

13 Quoted in Vidler, op cit, p74.

14 Richard Foreman, *Unbalancing Acts*, Pantheon (New York), 1992, p68.

15 Tschumi, op cit, p125.

16 Henri Lefebvre, *Critique of Everyday Life*, John Moore (trans), Verso (London/New York), 1991, p11.

17 Kaye, op cit, p195.

18 Ibid.

19 Ibid, p201.

20 Lefebvre, op cit, p155.

The Bastille Dances, *OPPOSITE: Barcelona, 1989; London, 1989; Cherbourg, 1989; FROM ABOVE:* The Bastille Dances, *Cherbourg, 1989;* Cuckoo, *London, 1987*

SUSAN NIGRA SNYDER AND ALEX WALL
EMERGING LANDSCAPES OF MOVEMENT AND LOGISTICS

Two jack-knifed tractor-trailer trucks, one on the Walt Whitman bridge and the other on Interstate 95, have closed Center City Philadelphia for the morning rush hour. It is the third such closing in the last three weeks.

Newark International Airport (the second busiest airport serving the New York metropolitan region) is closed for twenty-four hours due to the crash and burning of a Federal Express cargo jet.

The Teamsters Union threatens a strike against the United Parcel Service: other national and international carriers admit that they do not have the capacity to cover the increased load.[1]

What all of these incidents have in common is that they interrupted the 24-hour flow of goods along the nation's transport infrastructure. More goods need to go to more places more quickly because our consumption together with spatially fragmented modes of manufacturing require these accelerated flows. The varied origins and destination of these goods, the amount of information needed to process them, and the evolution of different kinds of services to expedite these flows together put a premium on distribution. Although the 'front-stage' of our consumption culture[2] – a landscape of shopping centres, malls, outlet centres, big box stores, cities of tourism; as well as the virtual world of advertisements, television, home television shopping and Internet commerce – has recently been recognised by the design professions, behind this frontal landscape of consumption is the less celebrated landscape of distribution systems – still little acknowledged by architecture and design.

The distribution landscape, domain of the logistics industry,[3] is where information and technology intervene with the physical bulk of goods at ports, rail yards, air cargo and truck depots. The development of just-in-time[4] manufacturing requires control of material that is dispersed throughout this landscape: from small FedEx packages to large containers holding industrial and automobile parts, which, for example, must come physically together within a window of one hour or else an entire assembly line will be closed for the day. Mail-order catalogues, television and Internet shopping are based on the fact that anything can be delivered directly to you. At the beginning of the process – probably at an industrial site – and most certainly at the final delivery to consumer or retailer, are trucks. These range from the tractor trailers that crowd the interstates to the vans that deliver to your front door. A zone of sheds and highways, animated by freight trains, trucks and vans moving along precisely controlled schedules: this is the distribution landscape. It is an emerging landscape of movement and logistics that is the ground for the figure of consumption.

The organisation of movement, infrastructure and new industrial ensembles has traditionally been at the fringes of the design

and planning professions. The effect of all of this traffic, however, threatens to overwhelm small towns and affect the economic viability and competitiveness of existing cities. In this essay we describe distribution landscapes at urban, regional and continental scale in order to examine the relationship between infrastructure and settlement. We will consider how the consequences of the myriad everyday acts of a consumption culture affect the process of urbanisation and generate new typologies of urban life. Our proposition is that, together with entertainment, leisure-tourism and science & technology research and development, distribution is a basis for new settlements and is precipitating new urban ensembles. First we will introduce this landscape by contrasting the new consumption sites of Manhattan with their main logistical support zone near Newark, New Jersey. We will then compare two fast growing settlements based on distribution. The first, Alliance, Texas is a community in formation set within the continuous suburbán settlement around Dallas-Fort Worth. The second, Laredo, Texas is a historic border town where the economy has always been based on cross-border traffic but which is now having to be restructured because of the NAFTA agreements between the US, Canada and Mexico.

The Front-Stage/Back-Stage Paradigm: New Consumption Needs New Distribution

The blocks of Times Square just north of 42nd Street have already been filling up with stores and theme restaurants, and they are thronged with people who seem to crave the notion of urban energy in a clean, controlled environment – a theme park version of the city itself.[5]

Writing about the striking transformation of Times Square and 42nd Street from a seedy zone of sex, drugs and crime into 'one of the hottest entertainment and shopping zones of any downtown in the United States', Paul Goldberger notes that the power of the marketplace – not the well-laid plans of civic activists, politicians and planners – has shaped a new kind of urban form. What the rebirth of this area reveals 'most of all is an evolution in the American city itself, from an environment driven primarily by business and commerce to one that exists mainly for tourism, entertainment and consumption.'[6] This environment of entertainment, tourism and leisure is by no means limited to Times Square. Evidence of these forces can be experienced at any one of the themed restaurants – Hard Rock Café, Planet Hollywood, etc – that have invaded the once staid 57th Street, or in one of the entertainment-retail stores on Fifth Avenue (such as Warner Bros Studio Store or Niketown NY) and finally, the 'malling' of SoHo or the soon-to-be Harlem USA on 125th Street. The consumption-distribution landscape is an integral part of the urban figure. The cleanliness, control and potentially ludic experience – adapted from the precedent of the shopping mall – are not only becoming prevalent but are expected by tourists and visitors to city centres. For the moment, Times Square may be the best-known

The back-stage of Manhattan is the distribution landscape of Port Newark which combines air cargo (Newark Airport), land transport (New Jersey Turnpike and secondary roads), rail (Conrail) and port facilities (warehouses and shipping terminals)

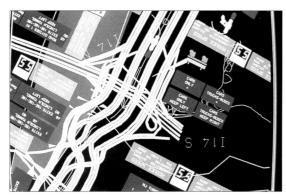

Computer image of a dynamic map from the Automatic Surveillance and Control System of the New Jersey Turnpike. Managers monitor traffic volume and flow interruptions from a central control point

World Trade Center, New York, seen across a landscape of trucks

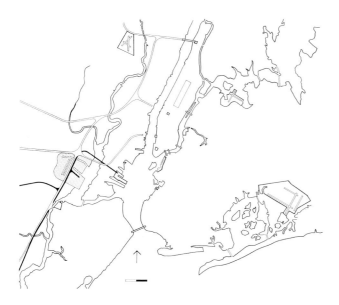

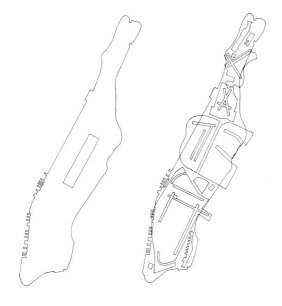

FROM ABOVE: New York Metropolitan Area, part plan, dot screen indicates Newark Airport and the Port Newark-Port Elizabeth zone; Manhattan island with superimposed Port Authority sites

example of a new consumption-entertainment district but many cities are developing downtown district legislation that will produce similar results.

What characterises these places of tourism, entertainment and consumption is the clear separation of front- and back-stage regions. In the case of Manhattan, the purity of the front-stage experience in Times Square noted by Goldberger is supported by a back-stage area that handles the movement of goods from arrival in the New York City region to the consumption destination. Some 11 miles to the southwest of Manhattan is perhaps the largest and most visible of distribution landscapes. Flanking the New Jersey Turnpike and the main east-coast Conrail freight line, both running from north to south, are Newark International Airport to the west, with its expanding air cargo and air courier services; and the Port Newark-Port Elizabeth Shipping Terminals, to the east. From the view of the cars and trucks driving along the Turnpike, this landscape appears to writhe with the movement of jets, cranes, cargo ships and freight trains. Here, according to Ken Spahn of the Port Authority, is the 'only place on earth where all major modes of transport are within a quarter of a mile of each other.'

While the components of this giant ensemble – airport, highways, port and rail yards – appear to be traditional industrial sites, the increasingly time-sensitive demands of global business and the limitation of a restricted site have caused these components to be in a state of continuous innovation and experimentation; the port was, for example, in 1956, the birthplace of containerisation, which created the basis of intermodality by reorganising road, rail and sea freight traffic around the module of the 20- and 40-foot-long container. Today, container movements are controlled by the Global Positioning System, which enables the colourful and apparently randomly arranged mountains of containers to be stacked according to their destination and location in the ship. The logistics area near Newark is an example of an ever more dense and interrelated urban industrial landscape that operates 24 hours a day. Rather like a stage set, this landscape must react to different and changing physical action, with ever more attention being drawn to the design and choreography of the surface.

The Port Authority of New York and New Jersey,[7] which includes four airports, ten port sites and six bridges and tunnels, must be highly responsive to trends in consumption and global manufacturing. It is a network which must by design integrate movement into the dense urban and suburban landscape of a region of 17 million people.[8] More than a service element, the infrastructure of the Port Authority is the most visible element of

Warner Bros, Studio Store, 57th Street and Fifth Avenue, New York

Hermes, 57th Street, New York

the city as a network of flows. Not surprisingly, the gross area of the major elements of the Port Authority is roughly the size of Manhattan.

The Intersection of Information and Goods: A New Urban Typology

Alliance is the trading capital of tomorrow, emerging from the North Texas prairie; a vital centre of international commerce linked to the world not by waterways, but by multiple transport systems.[9]

On a regional scale, new infrastructures are providing an armature for the growth of communities, both planned and unplanned. Unlike the Port Authority (9,700 acres), which is sandwiched between existing communities and attached to the waterways of New York, the land port of Alliance, covering 8,300 acres is built on what the developers call 'raw land', inexpensive and unencumbered land that lies between working cattle range and farmland. Its location is strategic both continentally and locally. It lies in the middle of the centroid of the North American Free Trade Area and, regionally, at the junction of two growth vectors: the first, running northwest from central Dallas through Las Colinas, Dallas-Fort Worth airport and the second, running due north from central Fort Worth along interstate 35W. Alliance, developed by Ross Perot, Jr, is an international business and transportation development that is based around the integration of several key systems: just-in-time manufacturing, surface transportation and global air freight.

Sited strategically in the centre of North America, it is composed of three elements. The first is the masterplanned industrial airport located near a newly built container yard of the Burlington Northern Santa Fe railroad's main line, both with immediate connections to the interstate highway system. Supporting this visible infrastructure is a telecommunications network of fibre-optic cable for voice, data and video transmissions. Second, around this infrastructure, which is the foundation on which the project relies and the support it needs for future growth, are 'Intermodal Business Parks', which are a planned response to global markets and international sourcing. The companies that are attracted to this distributional capability are typically companies with high-value, high-turnover inventories and multi-state or multi-national distribution systems such as Intel, American Airlines Maintenance and FedEx. Third, although only ten years old, Alliance is rapidly growing, adding adjoining residential neighbourhoods and shopping districts, including Glen Dale, one of the nation's fastest growing residential communities. The neat industrial parks and the bland well-off looking subdivisions

appear to be an image of the isolated suburb – yet the role of Alliance, the relationship between its elements and its planning, landscape and architecture are the result of a series of charettes that have included a provocative mix of designers and planners.[10]

The success of Alliance raises the question of where and how cities equipped for contemporary commerce might develop. The physical space necessary to couple light industry with intermodal transport infrastructure can't easily be developed in existing urban areas, where it would take too long to acquire sufficient land and be too expensive to retrofit sites with technologically up-to-date infrastructure. Traditionally, vital urban areas have been the product of civic authorities, but Alliance has been developed privately in co-operation with county, state and federal authorities. In the US, only private developers with access to global financing are equipped to mount such an enterprise and have it operational in such short time.

Alliance seems to be a working prototype for a new urban typology based on the intersection of information and goods.[11] T Allen McArtor, formerly of the Federal Aviation Administration, said that the US will need a dozen Alliances – a dozen new towns – to cope with the air cargo traffic that is the result of changes in consumption and manufacturing. Recalling the development of 'Technopoles' (science and technology research and development communities, described by Manuel Castells and Peter Hall),[12] the success of Alliance suggests another economic basis for residential communities – intermodal distribution centres combined with business parks. Both communities point the way to new urban typologies in a post-cold war era.

Border Towns: Unplanned Urbanism of Trade Agreements

Unlike most big border towns, the two Laredos don't manufacture much. What keeps their economies ticking is the vast merchandise flow, reflected in rows of warehouses outside of Laredo and a huge Wal-Mart distribution center. For the city's economy, 'God laid out the geography very well', says Gary G Jacobs, chairman of Laredo National Bank. 'The quickest way from Mexico City to Detroit is through Laredo.'[13]

Where Alliance was conceived and masterplanned through negotiations between a private developer with local and national authorities, some 400 miles south sustained unplanned development has been taking place in border towns that straddle the Rio Grande in response to the increased trade between the US and Mexico as a result of the NAFTA agreement.[14] According to the US census, Nuevo Laredo-Laredo, Reynosa-McAllen and

Residential development at Park Glen (from Alliance brochure)

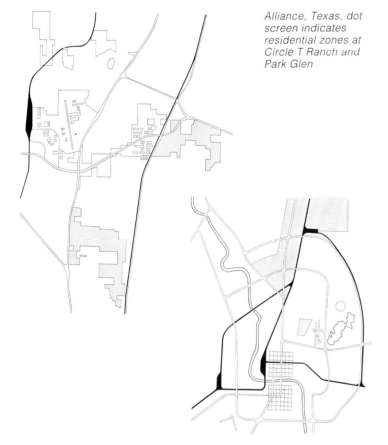

Alliance, Texas, dot screen indicates residential zones at Circle T Ranch and Park Glen

Matamoros-Brownsville are among the fastest growing North American cities. Principal among these is Laredo, which is the largest land port in the US and lies within 150 miles of the industrial centre of Monterey (Mexico), Corpus Christi seaport and San Antonio (both in Texas), allowing it to operate as a regional node of intermodal transport, logistics industries and warehousing. Laredo, whose grid plan was founded in 1767, has been alternately a Mexican, Texan and finally a double city straddling the border. It has become the second fastest growing American city in population and has increased 71 per cent in land size since 1989. Currently, traffic (more than 4,000 trucks a day) jams three bridges that cross the international border. Despite the dramatic proposals for new infrastructure – an expanded existing loop, a second outer highway loop, two new vehicle bridges (one exclusively for trucks), new freight railroad lines, container yards and a second rail bridge – Laredo is desperately trying to catch up with the increase in traffic.

Beyond the myriad urban, social, economic and political issues raised by these border towns, their transportation infrastructure has characteristics seen only in long-established, densely populated urban areas. Although two ring roads are not unusual around large metropolitan centres such as Atlanta and Washington, the inner and outer loops of Laredo will serve twin cities that together have a population of less than 500,000. The inner and outer loops will create a matrix not only for the Free Trade Zones but also new suburban residential communities. Unlike traditional industrial areas, the new sheds built for distribution and manufacturing are clean and set in landscaped 'campuses'. In Laredo, as at Alliance, the newest residential subdivisions are set between the industrial zones. Laredo and Nuevo Laredo are cities with a strong regional identity interwoven with an infrastructure that is scaled to continental traffic flows. The future quality of life in these cities relies on the successful design and integration of an infrastructure that otherwise answers the demands of factories and cities far away from its region.

The border region between Mexico and the US, from the Pacific Ocean to the Gulf of Mexico, has an economy larger than Poland and close to that of Thailand, with 11 million people and a gross regional product of $150 billion.[15] Growth of the new urban centres in this region is driven by a third world/first world juxtaposition: a cheap Mexican labour pool combined with US global competitiveness. The economies of the Mexican cities revolve around assembly plants, whereas their American counterparts deal in intermodal trade, logistics and warehousing. Together they are a locus of urban growth fuelled by a consumption-distribution economy in a region noted more recently for cattle ranges than traffic jams.

Cities of Flow and Interchange

As the pattern of urbanisation has changed from the radiocentric 19th- and 20th-century city to a dispersed regional settlement with multiple centres – distribution and consumption are altering traditional urban form in four ways: at street scale, by filling our roads with trucks working via electronic control on schedules that lead to intense traffic volume and accidents disrupting the daily urban system of every large city; at an urban scale, by transforming the front- and back-stage areas of cities; at a regional scale, by creating new urban structures that will provide the armature for the growth of new communities; and at a continental scale, by re-ordering the hierarchy of cities in a country's commerce. Slowly, national, regional and city maps are

Laredo, Texas and Nuevo Laredo, Tamaulipas, dot screen indicates new warehousing and free trade zones

Rancher with American Airlines maintenance hangar behind (from Alliance brochure)

being redrawn as the hierarchy of cities changes. What appears to be emerging is a back-stage group of cities – service cities driven by distribution – that serves, at regional and national scale, the front-stage cities that are the centres of business, culture, entertainment and leisure.

The forces generating this landscape have been overlooked either because they seem to be outside architecture or perhaps because we encounter them every day. When have movement and infrastructure been at the core of architects' concerns? 'Architects are not the engineers or technicians of the three great variables: territory, communication and speed.'[16] This statement by Foucault and our proposition that new centres of distribution may become the basis of new settlements would seem to float architecture uncomfortably between movement, infrastructure and the galloping commerce of consumption culture. But cities have always been commercially driven, and the appearance of new urban centres around networks of distribution would seem further evidence of Jane Jacobs' dictum that 'commerce is the engine of urbanity'. The military and industrial investment of the post-Second World War period that was the basis of the economy of both old cities and the new 'sunbelt' cities is receding. Leisure, research and development and – we propose with the examples of Alliance and Laredo – distribution are the bases for new settlements and the renovation of older settlements. Distribution differs by being reliant on intermodal transportation infrastructure which creates a significant impact on the landscape. Rather than the discrete or single-mode transportation favoured in previous models of garden cities or new towns, the settlements of the distribution landscape are distinguished by bold and diverse networks of movement. The matrix of movement and communications gives people the mobility and access to choose home, job, school, entertainment. As much as quality of life or economic imperative, access to this matrix is the basis of settlement.

Our examples may seem bound to the particular conditions of the US, or more locally, Texas, but the growth of communities devoted to the management and direction of flows of goods is taking place worldwide. The developers of Alliance intend to expand their logistics network of distribution service settlements and are currently seeking sites in Eastern Europe, the Middle East, South America and East Asia. But beyond the scope of this essay, the global extent and importance of these emerging landscapes of movement and logistics may soon be measured in the urban network arising in the Pearl River Delta of South China. Here a constellation of cities with its outer limits given by Hong Kong, Macau, Zhaoquing and Huizhou with Guangzhou at its core is devoted to finance, manufacturing and export – the commercial hinge between China and the world. At present, besides new roads and railways, five new intermodal container ports and five new airports with substantial air freight capacity are being built, all underpinned by a fibre-optic network. Will this discontinuous urban landscape of flow and interchange become, as Manuel Castells has asked, 'the most representative urban face of the 21st century?'.[17] Beyond understanding the locational logic of these new developments, we believe the distribution landscape is a testing ground for new kinds of settlement, spatial patterns and possibly an architecture where the shape of urban life is free to take on a new form.

Notes

Several individuals have contributed to our research in Laredo, including: Steven Fox of Rice University, Raphael Longoria of the University of Houston, Frank Rotnofsky and Viviana Frank of Frank Associates, Architects, Laredo, and Keith Selman of the Laredo Planning Department.

1 30 July 1997, Northeast Corridor between Philadelphia, Pennsylvania and Newark, New Jersey. News items from the *New York Times* and television evening news.

2 Culture and Consumption – People and goods are inextricably entwined. Goods make 'visible and stable the categories of culture', they 'make and maintain social relationships'. Goods, then, are the visible part of culture and consumption is the field in which culture is created, represented, reproduced, manipulated and challenged. Thus goods have no meaning without the human interaction that relates one to another. Goods may be considered markers of the social process, but meaning is embodied in the relationships between the markers, not in the commodity itself. Mary Douglas and Brian Isherwood, *The World of Goods*, WW Norton & Co (New York), 1982.

3 The Council of Logistics management defines logistics as, 'the process of planning, implementing, and controlling the efficient flow and storage of raw materials, in-process inventory, finished goods, services and related information from point of origin to point of consumption (including inbound, outbound, internal and external movements) for the purpose of conforming to customer requirements.'

4 Just-in-time (JIT) is a manufacturing/inventory control system that attempts to reduce inventory levels by co-ordinating demand and supply to the point where the desired item arrives just-in-time for use. The application of JIT production is rewriting the political and cultural map of organisations and a quite different set of working rules for managers and labour.

Chrysler receives 1,700 truck shipments a day – nine out of ten on JIT schedules. At a single GM plant, 23 trucks a day arrive from one particular supplier more than 200 miles away, and each truck must get there within a 15-minute window. L Lamm, 'Clean or Green: Political Correctness vs Common Sense in Transportation', *Vital Speeches*, vol XV, no 15, 15 May, 1994.

5 Paul Goldberger, 'The New Times Square: Magic That Surprised the Magicians', *The New York Times*, Tuesday 15 October, 1996.

6 Ibid.

7 The Port Authority of New York and New Jersey was created in 1921.

8 'In 1996 about six million tucks used interchanges 13A and 14 of the New Jersey Turnpike, destined primarily for Port Newark, Port Elizabeth and the Newark International Airport's Cargo facilities.'

9 Alliance Development Company.

10 The concept charettes in the 1980s included Julian Beinart, Gary Hack, Carl Hodges, Lester Thurow and Melvin Webber. The landscape charettes included Linda Jewel of Andropogon, Peter Rowland of the ASLA, Richard Haag, Ignacio Bunster of WRT and Laurie Olin. In 1996 some members of the original design charette were invited to critically reconsider the project to date. This charette included Ed Fenn from Gensler Associates, James Ingo Freed, Wes Jones, Stan Kellerberg of EDAW, Steve Polo and Kevin Shanley of SWA. Information received in telephone conversations with Isaac Manning, an architect and developer who is a member of Alliance Strategic Services.

11 'Was it significant that Skinner shared his dwelling with one who earned her living at the archaic intersection of information and geography? The offices the girl rode between were electronically coterminous – in effect, a single desktop, the map of distances obliterated by the seamless and the instantaneous nature of communication. Yet this very seamlessness, which had rendered physical mail an expensive novelty, might as easily be viewed as porosity, and as such created the need for the service the girl provided. Physically transporting bits of information about a grid that consisted of little else, she provided a degree of absolute security in the fluid universe of data. With your memo in the girl's bag, you knew precisely where it was; otherwise your memo was nowhere, perhaps everywhere, in that instant of transit.' William Gibson, *Virtual Light*, Penguin (London), 1993.

12 M Castells and P Hall, *Technopoles of the World*, Routledge, London, 1994.

13 Gery Smith and Elizabeth Malkin, 'The Border', *Business Week*, 12 May, 1997.

14 The North America Free Trade Agreement, signed in November 1993, promises to integrate the economies of Mexico, the United States and Canada.

15 Smith and Malkin, op cit.

16 Michel Foucault, 'Space, Knowledge and Power', *The Foucault Reader*, Pantheon, 1984, p244. Cited in B Webb, 'Engaging the Highway', *A+U*, no 289, October 1994.

17 Manuel Castells, 'The Information Age: Economy, Society and Culture', *The Rise of the Network Society*, vol I, Blackwell (Oxford), 1996, p409.

PATRICK KEILLER
THE DILAPIDATED DWELLING

Where I live, there seem to be two kinds of space. There is *new space*, in which none of the buildings are more than about ten years old, and there is *old space*, in which most of the buildings are at least 20 years old, a lot of them over 90 years old, and all are more-or-less dilapidated. Most of the *old space* is residential, but there are also small shops, banks, cafés, public houses, a health centre, a library, a social security office, schools and so on. Most of the *new space* is occupied by large corporations of one sort or another, a few of them international in scope, and it is not urban in the conventional sense. It includes retail sheds, supermarkets, fast food restaurants, a *Travel Inn*, a business park, distribution warehouses, tyre, exhaust and windscreen service centres. Most of these places have large car parks and security cameras. There is a lot of new space under construction, it goes up fast, and more is proposed. Buildings in *new space* do not have to last very long. In some of the older *new space* the original buildings have already been replaced by new ones.

The *old space* looks poor, even when it isn't. Much of it is poor, but when it isn't, the dilapidation is still striking. *Old space* appears to be difficult to maintain. A lot of the shops don't look as if they're doing very well. The cybercafé didn't last very long. The public institutions, if they are lucky, manage to maintain their buildings. The public lavatories are in a terrible state, though they are very photogenic. In the street, there is a fair amount of outdoor drinking, and according to the police who attend burglaries, there is a lot of heroin about. Many houses have burglar alarms. Some have cable television or Internet access.

At the moment, the residential property market is busy. There are always a lot of builders working, but they don't have the skills, the materials or the time to be particularly conscientious about anything beyond short-term performance. The conservationist is, as always, frustrated, and if anyone is responsible for the surfaces of *old space*, it is these builders and their clients.

In *old space*, apart from the smaller branches of banks and supermarket chains, the activities of large corporations are not very visible. A local estate agent, for example, is likely to be a major bank, building society or insurance company in disguise. Dilapidated houses are bought with mortgages from building societies, banks and other large corporations. A lot of small shops are franchises. The utility companies' installations are mostly underground, or in anonymous boxes which one tends not to notice. TV aerials and satellite dishes quickly blend with the domestic scene.

The dilapidation of *old space* seems to have increased, in an Orwellian way, with the centralisation of media and political power – by the disempowerment of local government, for instance. At the same time, experience of dilapidation is tempered by the promise of immediate virtual or imminent actual presence elsewhere, through telematics and cheap travel. As I stand at the bus stop with my carrier bags in the rain, I can window-shop cheap tickets to Bali, or contemplate Hong Kong, Antarctica or Santa Cruz as webcam images on my Nokia; or I could if I had one – the virtual elsewhere seems, if anything, most effective as mere possibility, as a *frisson*.

New space is mostly work space. An increasing proportion of 'economically active' people work in *new space*. Most of those who are not 'economically active' visit it fairly frequently, at least for the weekly shop, but they do not spend much time there. A very large number of people are not 'economically active' – they are physically or mentally ill, children, non-working parents, 'voluntary' carers, the unemployed, pop stars in waiting, unpublished novelists, the early or otherwise retired and other non-employed people. For these people, everyday surroundings are *old space*, and *old space* is mostly residential space – houses and flats. Residential space has a visiting workforce: the window cleaner, the decorator, the meter reader, the washing-machine engineer, the plumber, the small builder; as well as on-site earners slaving away at Christmas crackers, clothes, poetry or television research. Despite the talk about corporate homeworking and the long expected 'death of the office' most of the above are likely to be self-employed, and very few of them at all well paid. The real economic activity of residential space – housework, most of it involved with child-rearing – is not paid at all. It was recently estimated that the real value of housework in the UK is £739 billion, 22 per cent more than the current value of the country's GDP.[1] On average, people in the UK only spend 12 per cent of their total time in paid work.[2] Although unpaid, child-rearing is presumably the most significant of all economic activities in that it shapes – though not always directly – the values and attitudes of the next generation of wealth creators. *New space*, on the other hand, is mostly corporate, company-car territory. There are plenty of women working in *new space*, often in senior roles, but the structures and work patterns in these places do not easily accommodate active parenthood. Most flexible part-time work suited to the child-rearer pays under four pounds an hour.

In the UK, housing takes up around 70 per cent of urban land.[3] Its housing stock is the oldest in Europe with an average age estimated at about 60 years. A quarter of the stock was built before the end of the First World War.[4] There are about 24 million dwellings in all,[5] but in the last 20 years the rate of new house building has fallen to only 150,000 per year, largely because of the elimination of public-sector house building.[6] Most new housing is built by developers for sale on completion, and is widely criticised as unsophisticated and over-priced.[7] In other developed economies, house production occurs in different ways, but if the UK is taken as the extreme example of a *laissez-faire* system operating in a built-up landscape with a restricted land supply, one can perhaps discern a general tendency in that under advanced capitalism it is increasingly difficult to produce and maintain *the dwelling*. This is especially odd given that dwellings constitute the greater part of the built environment, that they are the spaces where most people spend most of their time, and where what is arguably the real 'work' of society is done. Modernity, it seems, is exemplified not so much by the business park or the airport, but by the dilapidated dwelling.

During the last 20 years or so domestic life has been transformed in many more-or-less electronic ways: supermarket distribution, increased unemployment and early retirement, programmable gas heating, computerised banking, new TV, video, audio, telecommunications, the personal computer and the Internet. Most of these things make it easier to stay at home, and many of them make it more difficult to go out, but the house itself has changed very little. The supermarkets, with computerised distribution and warehousing, and big trucks on modern roads, have transformed the UK's food market and shopping habits, for example creating a mass market in cosmopolitan food and drink that was previously only available in a few parts of London. In the same period, house production has merely declined, though, supermarkets now offer mortgages. For the corporate economy, the house seems to exist only as a given, a destination for sales of consumable materials and services.

There are many reasons why this might be the case. Firstly, houses last a long time. House building is also by its nature a very local undertaking, even for the largest producers. Wimpey, who claim to be the largest house builders in the world, only seem to advertise their developments locally. The tendencies in production that have brought Ford to the Mondeo – the world car – have never been widely applied to house production. Despite the best efforts of several generations of architects, houses are still not manufactured off site and are not generally susceptible to *distribution*. When they are available in this way, the purchaser is faced with the problem of finding a site on which to erect a single house, which in the UK is very difficult. IKEA have started to produce prefabricated dwellings, but so far they have erected the product themselves on their own development sites. There have been many impressive examples of factory-produced houses since the 18th century, but never in very large numbers.

In the middle of the 19th century, less than one per cent of the UK's national income was spent on house building.[8] Since before the time of Engels, industrial capitalism has been more usually accompanied by the production of large but insufficient numbers of poor-quality houses, palatial workplaces, and a small number of millionaires' mansions: the Rothschilds' houses of Mentmore and Waddesdon, for example, or Bill Gates' $50 million house on the shore of Lake Washington, near Seattle. It seems that, for capitalism, houses are a means of centralising wealth, rather than products to be distributed. In the last 100 years, relative to earnings, food and most manufactured goods have become much cheaper, but houses have become more expensive both to build and to buy. Industrial production has not been very successful at producing houses for the people who are otherwise

its consumers: most of the best housing developments of the last century or so seem to have been undertaken outside the market, by philanthropic employers, civic bodies or committed individuals and groups.

Since the late 1970s, 'housing' has been an unfashionable subject for architects and theorists. With a few notable exceptions – the architecture of Walter Segal, for instance – there has been very little house building of any architectural interest in the UK beyond a few one-off houses, these often for architects themselves. Among theorists and other writers, the very idea of *dwelling* has been recognised as problematic, for example:

Architects have long been attacking the idea that architecture should be essentially stable, material and anchored to a particular location in space. One of the main targets for those who would make architecture more dynamic is of course that bulwark of inertia and confinement, the outer casing of our dwelling place that we call a house. Which explains why, as early as 1914, the Futurists put their main emphasis – at least in theory – on the complex places of transit.

'We are . . . [the men] of big hotels, railway stations, immense roads, colossal ports, covered markets, brilliantly lit galleries . . .'

We are dissatisfied because we are no longer able to come up with a truly promising form of architecture in which we would like to live. We have become nomads, restlessly wandering about, even if we are sedentary and our wanderings consist of flipping through the television channels . . .'[9]

On the other hand:

Bridges and hangars, stadiums and power stations are buildings but not dwellings; railway stations and highways, dams and market halls are built, but they are not dwelling places. Even so, these buildings are in the domain of our dwelling. That domain extends over these buildings and yet is not limited to the dwelling place.[10]

In a culture in which so much of the space of work and transit is new, modern and professionally produced, but so much home space is old, amateurish and artlessly hand-made, one tends to forget that, like the industrial landscapes that inspired the modernist avant-garde, the corporate economy only exists because it has been able to develop global markets in the necessities and longings of domestic life. The dominant narratives of modernity – mobility and instant communication – appear to be about *work* and *travel*, not *home*. They are constructions of a work-oriented academic élite about a work-oriented business élite. However, as Saskia Sassen points out:

A large share of the jobs involved in finance are lowly paid clerical and manual jobs, many held by women and immigrants' . . . the city concentrates diversity. Its spaces are inscribed with the dominant corporate culture but also with a multiplicity of other cultures and identities. The dominant

Victoria Street, Reading, 'Reading in England was a sleepy biscuit- and beer-making town until it was invaded by decentralised offices from London and high-technology factories from California.'[18]

L to R: Rear of signs: 'COMING SOON ON THIS SITE, A WARNER BROTHERS 9-SCREEN MULTIPLEX CINEMA, OPENING EASTER 1996'

Bus shelter, Great Bridge Street, West Bromwich, 'For amid the Ridley Scott images of world cities, the writing about skyscraper fortresses, the Baudrillard visions of hyper-space . . . most people actually live in places like Harlesden or West Brom. Much of life for many people, even in the heart of the first world, still consists of waiting in a bus shelter with your shopping for a bus that never comes.'[19]

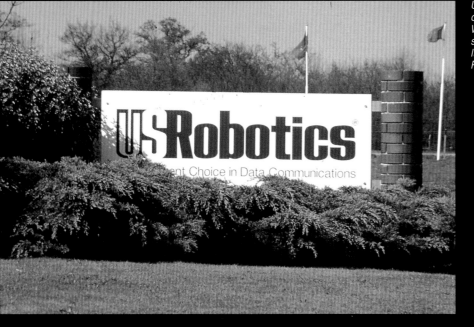

US Robotics, Winnersh Triangle business and distribution park, between Reading and Wokingham. Microsoft and Digital also have sites at Winnersh and Microsoft are building a large new site nearby at Thames Valley Park, Reading

and '40TH AND TESS PASSED IT. WELL DONE', opposite houses in Ripple Road, Dagenham – the A13 to Tilbury and the Dartford Tunnel

Sign to Midpoint distribution park, near Junction 18 of the M6 at Middlewich, Cheshire. Tesco has a 37,500-square-metre distribution centre at Midpoint, built in 1993; it has 33,000 pallet positions and a holding capacity of 43 million cases, or nine days' stock for 120 stores in an area which extends as far as Gateshead; each store receives between one and four deliveries per day

Images are frame enlargements from Robinson in Space (Patrick Keiller, 1997, 83 min), a BBC film distributed by the British Film Institute and available as a Connoiseur/Academy Video

culture can encompass only part of the city. And while corporate power inscribes non-corporate cultures and identities with 'otherness', thereby devaluing them, they are present everywhere. This presence is especially strong in our major cities which also have the largest concentrations of corporate power. We see here an interesting correspondence between great concentrations of corporate power and large concentrations of 'others'. It invites us to see that globalisation is not only constituted in terms of capital and the new international corporate culture (international finance, telecommunications, information flows) but also in terms of people and non-corporate cultures. There is a whole infrastructure of low-wage, non-professional jobs and activities that constitute a crucial part of the so-called corporate economy.[11]

Dwellings are rarely corporate space (see Billy Wilder's *The Apartment*). Are dwellings 'other'? The 'other' space in the city centres, where corporate power is concentrated, is usually the dwelling space of 'other' cultures and identities. The dwellings of corporate insiders are usually located at a distance, but even they live in homes that represent a level of investment per square metre that is only a fraction of that made in their workplaces. At the same time, domesticity is characterised by intimacy, the 'nearness' that Kenneth Frampton noted as increasingly absent from architecture,[12] presumably most of all from corporate architecture. Perhaps these qualities of domesticity are 'other' to the corporate economy, even in the homes of corporate insiders? Perhaps we are all *others* when we are at home?

> Marginality is today no longer limited to minority groups, but is rather massive and pervasive; this cultural activity of the non-producers of culture, an activity that is unsigned, unreadable and unsymbolised, remains the only one possible for all those who nevertheless buy and pay for the showy products through which a productivist economy articulates itself. Marginality is becoming universal. A marginal group has now become a silent majority.[13]

Heidegger's formulation of *dwelling* certainly sounds unfashionable in the late 20th century:

> *Only if we are capable of dwelling, only then can we build*. Let us think for a while of a farmhouse in the Black Forest, which was built some 200 years ago by the dwelling of peasants. Here the self-sufficiency of the power to let earth and heaven, divinities and mortals enter *in simple oneness* into things, ordered the house. It placed the farm on the wind-sheltered mountain slope looking south, among the meadows close to the spring. It gave it the wide overhanging shingle roof whose proper slope bears up under the burden of snow, and which, reaching deep down, shields the chambers against the storms of the long winter nights. It did not forget the altar corner behind the community table; it made room in its chamber for the hallowed places of childbed and the 'tree of the dead' – for that is what they call a coffin there: the *Totenbaum* – and in this way it designed for the different generations under one roof the character of their journey through time. A craft which, itself sprung from dwelling, still uses its tools and frames as things, built the farmhouse.[14]

This essay was invoked by Frampton towards the end of his *Modern Architecture – A Critical History* as a recognition of a quality of experience that many believed most modern building had lost. This loss being, they said, why many people had

rejected modern architecture, and why, perhaps, we have speculative house builders who build houses for sale that are supposed to resemble the tied cottages of Victorian farm workers.

Richard Sennett, in a lecture in 1992, pointed out that Heidegger neglected the *stupefying* nature of *dwelling*, and that in fact *dwelling* and *thinking* are antithetical. The creativity of cities, said Sennett, arises from their being sites of unresolved conflict between *thinking* and *dwelling*.

It is easy to poke fun at Heidegger's notion of dwelling – so nostalgic, so conservative, so *agricultural* – so at odds with a quasi-nomadic hunter-gatherer present as to be unhelpful, if not actually undesirable, especially in the context of his involvement with Nazism in the 1930s. Although the house he evokes is exemplary as a work of *architecture* (and has the required longevity), the social fabric – the *dwelling* – that produced it is almost unattainable, unsupportable, though perhaps not quite. In a letter responding to some of these questions, a friend wrote:

> Recently we visited together with students of architecture the small village Halen in Switzerland, designed by Atelier 5, still located in an unspoiled forest. The extremely narrow terraced houses with small private courtyards and a central public place, built more than 30 years ago, were in a perfect state, well kept, partly modernised (insulation of the external walls). The common installations like the shop in the piazza, the petrol station, the swimming pool and the tennis lawn were still working and in good condition. The community, now living in the houses, were to a high percentage the children and grandchildren of the initial owners. They have returned after they first had left the houses of their parents.

Frampton has described Halen as, 'one of the most seminal pieces of land settlement built in Europe since the Second World War . . . a model for reconciling development with place-creation and the maintenance of ecological balance'.[15] If Halen represents something approaching the modern attainment of Heidegger's *dwelling*, as Frampton seems to suggest by his subsequent reference to Heidegger, it is intriguing to learn that many of those who live there occupy the houses of their parents.

We are more familiar with this kind of *dwelling* in the context of its loss. In a World Service radio interview, a Bosnian refugee in Mostar longs to return to his house in Stolac, 50 kilometres away, from which he was evicted by his Croat neighbours, even though the town is still under Croat control: 'My family has lived in Stolac for centuries . . . I love the smell of the river . . .' For most of us, there is another kind of *dwelling*:

> The purpose of this work is to . . . bring to light the models of action characteristic of users whose status as the dominated element in society (a status that does not mean that they are either passive or docile) is concealed by the euphemistic term 'consumers'.

> In our societies, as local stabilities break down, it is as if, no longer fixed by a circumscribed community, tactics wander out of orbit, making consumers into immigrants in a system too vast to be their own, too tightly woven for them to escape from it.

> Increasingly constrained, yet less and less concerned with these vast frameworks, the individual detaches himself from them without being able to escape them and can henceforth only try to outwit them, to pull tricks on them, to rediscover, within an electronicised and computerised megalopolis, the 'art' of the hunters and rural folk of earlier days.[16]

If we think of ourselves as *consumers* in this way, perhaps our difficulties with housing are easier to understand. How is housing *consumed*?

In the context of the urban home in the UK, De Certeau's notion of 'tactics' as a response to the predicament of being a consumer evokes not so much do-it-yourself – currently a bigger market in the UK than new house building – but the way that the character of the public-sector housing 'estate' is changing 'as local stabilities break down'. In Inner London and elsewhere, the system of allocating public-sector housing on a basis which reflected its philanthropic origins in the 19th century has been fractured since the 1970s by ideas like the 'hard-to-let' flat, by the 'right to buy' and by an increase in social mobility generally. Public-sector housing was financed by 60-year loans, and was often designed by critically respected architects. It aimed to be of far better quality than that produced by the private sector. Often the more architecturally ambitious developments (including some influenced by the model of Halen) were difficult to build and were regarded as problematic early in their history, but some of them have aged well and have gradually accumulated populations who find them attractive as places to live.

Whatever the wider implications, perhaps architects can take some comfort from this. The notion of 'the everyday' in architecture offers a welcome relief from conventional interpretations of architectural value, especially in a culture where most 'everyday' building is not produced with much architectural intention, but it seems to affirm the spatial quality and detail of architects' architecture where it exists. Similarly, the subjective transformations of spatial experience characteristic of both the Surrealists and the Situationists might seem to promise a way of transcending assumptions of spatial poverty, of transforming 'even the most colourless localities', as Breton said of Aragon's 'spellbinding romantic inventiveness',[17] but in practice both groups were quite selective about the sites they favoured. In the long run, spatial and other architectural qualities seem to survive, though often not in the way that was expected.

The UK's new Labour government seems to be prepared to leave house building to the private sector, even for the showcase 'Millennium Village' development next to the dome at Greenwich. The long-term success of the Lansbury estate in Poplar, which was built as the housing showcase for the 1951 Festival of Britain, has not prompted Labour to recall that its commitment to public-sector housing produced so many internationally acclaimed housing developments between 1945 and the early 1970s. Not long before the 1997 election, Richard, Lord Rogers, newly ennobled in preparation for a Labour victory, presented an edition of the BBC's *Building Sites* – in which celebrities present favourite buildings – for which he selected the former London County Council's Alton Estate at Roehampton in southwest London – the Modern Movement landmark of 1952-59. This timely endorsement of the heroic period of public-sector housing seems not to have awakened any enthusiasm among members of the new government.

So far (at the time of writing), Labour has said little about housing, but appears to be giving tacit support to various private-sector proposals for 'super-villages': 5,200 new houses near Peterborough; 3,000 at Micheldever in Hampshire; between 5,000 and 10,000 houses west of Stevenage; 3,300 houses in three new villages near Cambridge. The latter have been 'masterplanned' by the architect Terry Farrell for a consortium of Alfred McAlpine, Bryant and Bovis in 'Cambridgeshire vernacular', an attempt to create 'a traditional village, with village greens with cricket pavilions, local shops and pubs' and a 69,677 square metre business park. With or without cricket pavilions, none of these developments sound as if they will have much chance of either 'reconciling development with place-creation and the maintenance of ecological balance' or attempting to reconfigure the house as something approaching a successful industrial product.

Labour's belief in finding an accommodation with the market seems to preclude a revival of public-sector house building on anything like its former scale, but the history of house building suggests that the market will never be able to modernise *dwelling* on its own, and Labour is committed to modernisation. If there is to be any possibility for a more promising approach to *dwelling*, it is very unlikely to come from the conventional house-building industry. Some of the most successful house-building projects in the UK during the last two decades have been non-commercial initiatives which included houses for sale. In the Netherlands, the government's VINEX policy aims to build 800,000 dwellings by the year 2,000 in a planned programme with commitments to credible architectural design and environmental and transport policies. This approach produces domestic architecture for sale of a quality that house buyers in the UK can only dream about. If house production in the UK is to undergo any kind of consumer-led reform, it looks as if this can only happen in the context of similar collectivist initiatives.

Notes

1 Announcement by the Office for National Statistics, reported in *The Guardian*, October 7 1997. The figure is for unpaid work valued at the same average rate as paid employment.

2 Ibid.

3 Michael Ball, *Housing and Construction: A Troubled Relationship*, Policy Press (Bristol), 1996, p1.

4 Philip Leather and Tanya Morrison, *The State of UK Housing*, Policy Press (Bristol), 1997, p21.

5 Central Statistical Office, *Regional Trends*, 1995 edition, HMSO (London), p94.

6 Ball, op cit, p7.

7 Ibid, p47.

8 Ibid, p8.

9 Florian Rötzer, 'Space and Virtuality: Some Observations on Architecture', in *The Future of Space*, Bernd Meurer (ed), Campus Verlag (Frankfurt/New York), 1994, pp205-206, 217.

10 Martin Heidegger, 'Building Dwelling Thinking', in *Poetry, Language, Thought*, Albert Hofstadter (trans), Harper and Row (New York), 1975, p145.

11 Saskia Sassen, 'Economy and Culture in the Global City', in *The Future of Space*, Campus Verlag (Frankfurt and New York), 1994, p74.

12 Kenneth Frampton, *Modern Architecture – A Critical History*, Thames and Hudson (London), 1980, p312.

13 Michel de Certeau, *The Practice of Everyday Life*, Steven Randall (trans), University of California Press (Berkeley), 1984, p.xvii. *L'Invention du quotidien, 2. Habiter, cuisiner*, by Luce Giard and Pierre Mayol, was published in French in 1980, and deals, writes Steven Randall, with 'a "fine art of dwelling", in which places are organised in a network of history and relationships, and a "fine art of cooking", in which everyday skill turns nourishment into a language of the body and the body's memories.'

14 Heidegger, op cit, p160.

15 Frampton, op cit, p311.

16 De Certeau, op cit, ppxi-xii, xx, xxiv.

17 André Breton, quoted from a radio interview in Simon Watson Taylor's introduction to his translation of Louis Aragon, *Paris Peasant*, Picador (London), 1980, p10.

18 Peter Hall, 'The Geography of the Fifth Kondratieff', in *Uneven Re-development*, Doreen Massey and John Allen (eds), Hodder & Stoughton (London), 1988, p52.

19 Doreen Massey, 'A Place Called Home?', in *Space, Place and Gender*, Polity Press (Cambridge), 1994, p163.

GILLIAN HORN

EVERYDAY IN THE LIFE OF A CARAVAN

The image of row upon row of shiny boxes hugging the landscape is a familiar one across Britain. Rural, seaside or post-industrial, the pattern is the same: a glimmering plateau of roofs that hover ten feet above the ground. Hundreds of thousands of caravans[1] huddled together in holiday caravan parks form these landscape blankets which, through their proliferation, may well seem commonplace and ordinary.

The caravan park is perhaps exemplary of the *everyday*: its caravans mass-produced with cheap materials, low technology and largely unskilled labour; its owners and users predominately working- and lower-middle-class couples and families; and its facilities unpretentious and unexceptional in their planning and landscaping. From the gnomes and busy lizzies around their borders to their chintz and wipe-down, wood-look interiors, caravans, their parks and inhabitants, must surely be the epitome of the everyday in our constructed environment.

Unaspiring, unglamorous and unwelcome in our upwardly mobile communities, the caravan is treated with little more than disdain. Why is it that caravans are so consistently denigrated by the middle classes? Why do they have no status, allure, or cultural value to us? Why do we dismiss them as common and everyday? I would argue that, under closer scrutiny, the caravan reveals itself as a far from ordinary dwelling and the caravan park as an extraordinary place; a place where people escape from the everyday and reinvent it as a realised fantasy.

The status of the caravan holiday home is an ambiguous one: it is used like a home but not as home and although it feels like a home it doesn't look like one. Neither vehicle nor house, yet transportable and habitable, the caravan falls between the 'mobile' and 'home' of its namesake. Even its terminology is indeterminate: caravan, mobile home, static, holiday home and leisure home all describe the corrugated aluminium or plastic clad prefabricated unit that sits on a steel chassis two feet off the ground, revealing the incongruously small wheels which mark its identity and signify its ambiguity.

It is the flickering sense of 'home' captured in the caravan which lends it its particular qualities. The caravan is like a toy; a discrete box with openings through which you can see life-sized domestic interiors that have somehow been squeezed into its unyielding case. There is a thinness about caravans which is both literal and metaphorical; the interiors are the stage sets of home, with images of homeliness veneered onto every surface.[2]

There is a discernible formula behind the caravan interior founded on iconic images of home which are grafted together to form a ready-made house-set: a distillation of the domestic suburban interior. The living/dining area centres around the hearth with display mantel, TV stand and book/knick-knack shelf. To one side of this core is a glass-doored, perhaps even mirror-backed, drinks/ornament display cabinet and to the other is a framed or flute-edged mirror. The caravan interior is dominated by the presence of a large bay window at the end of the living

area, recalling the archetypal suburban home. Built-in, soft seating with warm patterned covers wraps around this bay which occupies the entire width of the caravan, exaggerating the sense of space. The aluminium windows are netted and framed by heavy curtains and pelmets, colour co-ordinated with the upholstery. The master bedroom boasts a vanity unit with fitted, decorative mirror, shelves and fitted cupboards. The kitchen comes with full-sized appliances with tile-effect vinyl covering the visible floor and wall surfaces. Elsewhere, fitted carpets and patterned wallpaper-effect walls complete the ensemble.

Emphasis is given to these homely constructs through their relative scale to the actual size of the interior – the footprint of a six-berth caravan can be as small as 27 square metres – with not a square inch of surface left unstyled or referentially ambiguous. These features become exaggerated in the compact space creating an appearance of home that seems both more ideal and more tangible than home itself, whose associations with the ideal have become lost in the everyday realities of home life.

There is a sense of the uncanny in the caravan that extends beyond its resonance with 'the unhomely' (the literal translation of *das Unheimliche*). The holiday caravan is more of a satellite addition to the home than a substitute for it, but it is enough like home to throw into question the very identity and value of what 'home' is. The caravan works like a Freudian double to the home.[3] The caravan's theatrical projection of homeliness creates a superficial reflection of its source, the home, and through this discordant familiarity throws suspicion on the security of the home ideal. This effect destabilises the myth of the home as a protected place of retreat that enables a return to a state of satiated need. It exposes the home itself as a substitute, rather than source, for a desired state of unity; in playing with the culturally ingrained symbols, ideals and dictates of behaviour associated with home, the caravan thus poses a threat to the validity of the myth of the home by exposing it as such.

Whilst the caravan interior is directly modelled on the generic, suburban home interior, the exterior makes no gesture towards the imagery or associated ideologies of the suburban house. Unlike the suburban house which can be read as an integrated facet of an articulated streetscape, the caravan is a dislocated object in the uninterrupted landscape of the caravan park. The dichotomy of the veneered, home-narrative construction of the interior to the pared down, no-frills vehicular narrative of the exterior is extreme. No attempt is made on the exterior to disguise the physical reality of the caravan. Nor is there any attempt to assume a house-like identity in its description; caravans are all sold and referred to by their exterior dimensions (in feet) which are inscribed on the cladding. Whereas the interior of the caravan exposes ideals and collective assumptions about the physical and ideological nature of home through its intentional, motivated similarities, the exterior reveals some of the inherent assumptions in our ideological constructions of 'house', 'home' and 'community' in its radical departure from them.

The signification of the house as the *real* home is made apparent in the exterior treatment of residential park homes in comparison to their second cousin, the caravan. Park homes, sold and sited for year-round living as primary residences, are essentially caravans that are dressed up to look like homes from the outside, rather than merely fitted out to feel like homes inside. Their pitched roofs, textured render walls and brick skirts all imply permanence on the site and an outward image of a secure home. For these everyday homes, mobility and temporality are disguised and denied, redolent as they are with associations of transience, instability, gypsies and social outcasts, in an attempt to display idealised virtues of stability, stasis and permanence that are deemed to be implicit within the typology of the suburban house. This identification with the grounding of the house signals a desire to belong in society and can be read as a gesture towards accepting its codes for belonging.

The interior layout of the caravan is arranged under the orthodox principle that separates private sleeping and washing areas from more open, cooking, dining and socialising areas. Although these boundaries are less rigid in the compact space of the caravan than in the conventional home, the established hierarchies of privacy are accepted. The siting of the caravan within the park, however, radically departs from these conventions and bears little relation to its suburban counterpart. Between the street and the suburban house, there is a sequence of thresholds leading from the public road, kerb and pavement to the semi-public fence, gate, path and drive to the semi-private planted border, garage, porch, doormat and solid front door. This serves to establish the physical and psychological detachment and privacy of the suburban home. In the caravan park, however, the physical boundaries tend to lie only at the site perimeter. There are rarely any material boundaries separating the caravans, or designating their proprietal limits, other than an access road, some occasional planting and the caravans themselves. Nor is there the elaborate sequence of barriers that, in a suburban house, serves to protect the domain of the home. In the caravan park these codes of ownership and separation are reduced to Tarmac strip, swathe of grass (*not* lawn), perimeter planting around the caravan and steps up to a plain glass door. Each caravan has its own territory for which it is responsible, but this area is not marked, with the effect that the control and codes of this territory become blurred and its boundaries become socially respected rather than physically enforced.

This dissolution of boundaries within the caravan park has the further effect of merging the positing, and protocols, of 'fronts' and 'backs' in and around the caravan. The distinction of 'front' and 'back' dominates the pattern of conventional housing in which the front garden, used for public display (of taste, order, wealth), is separated by the house from the back garden, used for private occupation. In turn, the front of the house, through its

FROM ABOVE: Caravan park in Essex; caravans in a Kent caravan park; caravan undercroft

Living area of Atlas' Status Super caravan, 1997

Living area of ABI Leisure Homes' Montrose caravan, 1997

Living area of Cosalt Holiday Homes' Monaco Super caravan, 1997

weighted balance of wall to window, offers privacy for those within whilst maintaining the opportunity to observe those without, and the back of the house, protected by the buffer of the private garden, can afford to open and extend the home outside. In the caravan park, however, there are no front gardens for show and back gardens for (secret) pleasure; no front doors for visitors and back doors for family. Instead there are areas of occupation which are inhabited according to the orientation of each caravan on its pitch and the relative positions of neighbours, cars and sun. Deck chairs, plastic tables and cars all assume equivalence as accessories to the caravan park landscape.

It appears that the whole caravan park is a 'back', the boundary and formality of 'fronts' beginning at the park entrance, the threshold to the everyday, 'real' world. In the backyard of the site, the usual guards of the occupants waiver and their sense of propriety shifts. People live out what is commonly considered to be a nostalgic ideal of community: friendly, connected and informal. Weekend or holiday lives become what people would like their everyday lives to be, but it precisely because caravan life is not *every*day life that this fantasy is made possible.

In bringing the act of living out an imaginary everyday closer to its ideal, the caravan becomes more homely, in its lived experience, than the home itself. The caravan thereby transcends its role as a mere symbol of homeliness and takes on the function of a reality. In effect, through this shift in the status of the imaginary and reality, the 'real' home becomes secondary to the 'fantasy' home of the caravan. Indeed, its invisible presence becomes a critical support to the realigned set of relationships. By virtue of negotiating the balance between reality and illusion, the ordinary and extraordinary, such a fantasy of the everyday is able to be constructed and lived out in caravan parks.

Caravan parks are generally only open for nine months of the year, so it is assumed, and more often is the case, that the occupants all have 'real' homes elsewhere. The assumption that there is, out of view, a conventional property sited in a conventional community, following its conventional codes, is critical to the success of the reality of the caravan park community. The presence of an absent double to the caravan allows the necessary freedom, within the park, to detach from the stringent assessments which we use to form our 'real', but in effect mythical, communities outside.[4] These so-called communities are based on superficial identification rather than shared experience. There is a desire to belong (and a fear of exclusion), but 'belonging' is judged by criteria that are based on wealth, race, class and social status, evaluated through a set of associative codes attached to property. The affluent, acquisitive middle classes, to which our society aspires, display their mythical virtues of being proper, responsible and just, through their property which is symbolically loaded with their projected identities. Caravans bypass this identification process; they are not valued as property and are not considered as secure financial assets that have taken a lifetime's hard work to accrue. In this sense, they are not considered to represent a demonstration of commitment, faith and investment in a community.

The irony is that it is the caravan park which might come closest to being a community. That membership is voluntary, association is temporal and social pretences are removed offers the chance to relate, as needs be, through actual, lived, common ground, with some of the prejudices (which protect us from the risks of interaction), attached to our real, everyday lives put aside. Perhaps, then, in the caravan park's realised ideal of community, created through an imaginary construct of the everyday, there is an example and lesson for us all.

Notes

1 'Caravan' is used here as a generic term to describe semi-permanent, off-site manufactured holiday-homes-on-wheels.

2 Nothing is quite as it first appears, the seams between ceiling panels of the caravan are edged with timber to look as if they hold up the caravan as beams hold up a cottage.

3 Sigmund Freud, 'The Uncanny', *Art and Literature*, vol 14, The Penguin Freud Library, Penguin (Harmondsworth), 1990.

4 Richard Sennett discusses 'the myth of the purified community' in his book *The Uses of Disorder: Personal Identity and City Life,* Pelican Books (Los Angeles), 1973.

SARAH WIGGLESWORTH AND JEREMY TILL
TABLE MANNERS

Our Dining Table

Four stories; four different narratives about a project whose subject is the relationship between work and home.

Story 1. The Dining Table
Faced with a blank sheet of paper and a couple of buildings to design, where do you start? Any novelist will tell you: write about what you know. What we know is that living and working from the same building means our two lives (work and home) are never easily distinguished, but rather are irrevocably intertwined. An architect's response to this might be: separate the two physically; clarify zones; keep activities distinct; apply order. The person who lives and works there knows this is impossible. The Dining Table shows why.

The Dining Table sits in the centre of our 'parlour', the front room of our terraced house. On it stand items of everyday domestic use such as salt cellar and pepper mill, vases of flowers, fruit bowl and candlesticks. On an average day it collects the detritus of domestic life: letters and mailshots, magazines, keys, bike lights and small change. At regular intervals it becomes the site for meals, gathering over time the marks of the food and drink spilled on its surface. At other times it is the venue for office meetings, because our office is not large enough to accommodate more than four

people. At such times it is to be found scattered with pieces of paper, models, drawings, pens and other evidence of office life. The surface retains the patina of time, the traces of past events indelibly etched into the surface. At no time can the Dining Table be said exclusively to represent one side of life more than another. This ambiguity is an essential motif in the reinvention of the new house and office. In this process, the Dining Table itself is the starting point for the project, acting as a trope for the design of spaces which inscribe home and work simultaneously.

The Dining Room in the new scheme occupies a space which positions the table ambiguously between the house and the office, recognising the claims of both to the use of its surface. At times the space is used as a conference room for the office, the place of official business. At other times it can be united with the house and plays the role of the formal dining room.

Above the table hangs a chandelier of broken milk bottles: discarded domestic artefacts fashioned into a status symbol. The chandelier signifies the formal nature of this space; yet as a mediating world it symbolises the conditions of real life, reminding us in the gentlest way that we have several identities, often co-existent.

Our Dining Table

The Lay of the Table

An architectural ordering of place, status and function
A frozen moment of perfection.

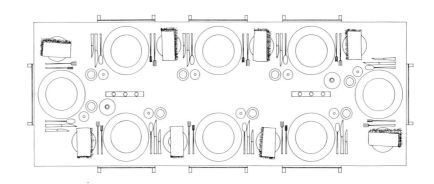

The Meal

Use begins to undermine the apparent stability of the (architectural) order
Traces of occupation in time
The recognition of life's disorder.

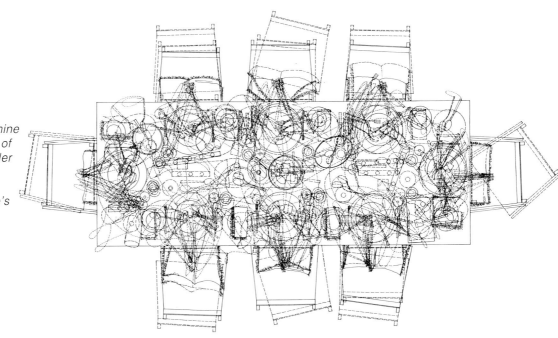

The Trace

The dirty tablecloth, witness of disorder
Between space and time
The palimpsest.

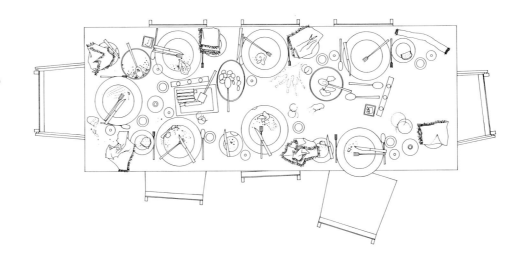

The Lay of the Plan

Recognition of an/other system of order
Domestic clutter filling the plan(e).

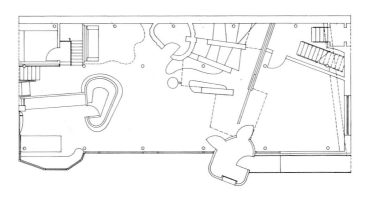

These four drawings are an exploration of the idea of order in architecture. They document the transformation of the plane of the ordered dining table into the plan of the house. The sequence begins with the table in readiness for an evening meal.

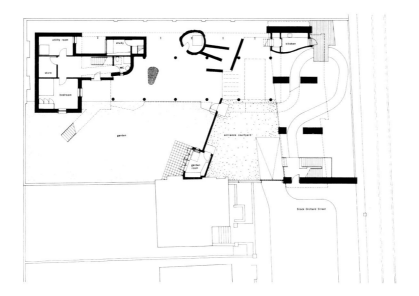

Ground Floor Plan
Open space under the floor plan of the house. Chickens foraging in the bark chips. Rude nature and a pile of compost amongst a grid of columns. The rhythm of residual party walls held captive in wire cages. A ramp which pauses to register the 10.05 to Edinburgh as it passes the trembling train spotting terrace. Bike sheds and back doors.

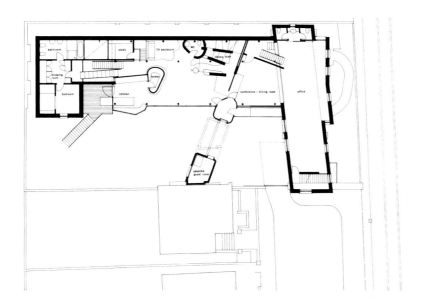

First Floor Plan
Bürolandschaft *for the home. Attic loft for the office. Dining/Conference room as hall. Shiny columns against furry blobs and hairy walls. Cooling larder and warming hearth. A sandbag wall peels away to give momentary glimpses of whistling trains. Narnian wardrobe as a place of transition. The plan comes to rest as we go to bed. Guests docking with the lobby Mir-style; sliding like a snail back along the garden wall. No slimy trails.*

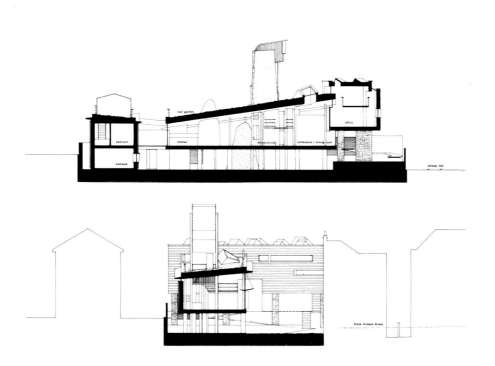

Section
A bed inside a cupboard. Planes punctured by projections. Wild straw-berries growing on a tilted roof. A tower whose bricks are books, demanding exertion. A lookout post, a signal box, whose roof slips away under starry skies. A ramp climbing through ruined walls.

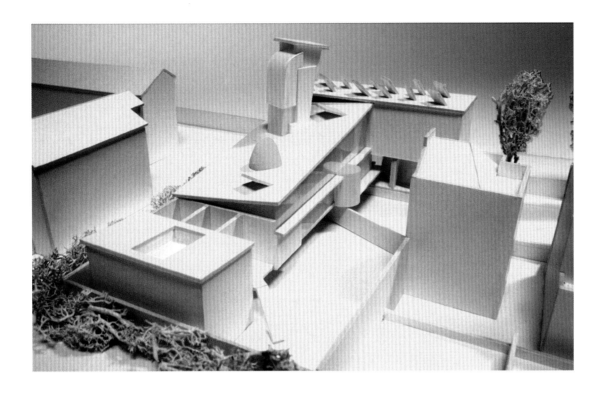

Story 2. Technologies of the Everyday

The technology of building is assumed to 'progress' towards increasing sophistication. The meaning of sophistication is: greater reliance on Western, energy-rich, complex, industrialised processes. It is not considered progressive to use resource-spare, readily-available by-products from existing industries. Technology transfer is alright as long as it is a transfer to architecture from industries like aeronautical engineering, boat building or nanotechnology: cutting-edge manufacturing to which earthbound architecture aspires.

In contrast, all the innovative forms of building used in the house and office come under the category we have named 'reverse technology transfer'. In this transaction we adopt deliberately simple technologies to show how architecture has locked itself into patterns of thinking which are inscribed into its ideology and its legal codes (building regulations, for example). Our technologies are obvious and easy to construct; they can be performed by people without great prior knowledge and they make use of existing and ready-at-hand materials. They are even fun.

Gabions The Office is a narrow strip of floorspace which sits on four thick walls made of gabions. Gabions are normally used as retaining walls alongside river banks or motorways, cages of galvanised steel wire into which are packed stones, rocks or, in our case, lumps of concrete recycled from the site. They are physically too big for their job but why should engineering always be about the minimal? Why shouldn't it be about excess?

Sandbags The Office faces a main-line railway. The wall fronting the line is defended from this aural invasion, just as we did in wartime, by stacking sandbags against the force of the intruder. Civil defence authority hessian bags are filled with a mix of sand and a small amount of cement. After some months and some rain, the cement goes off. Later, when the hessian rots and falls away in shreds the form of the bag, complete with the imprint of the weave on its surface, remains.

Strawbales Thick, insulating and light to handle, straw bales are the perfect material with which to make a north wall. Strawbales wrap the house on these faces, coddling the bedroom wing from head to foot like a feather-filled coverlet. While they can be used as a load-bearing system, we are using them as infill between timber trusses. Both walling material and insulation rolled into one, the bales are clad in a rainscreen made of transparent polycarbonate, celebrating the beauty of the natural product. The tension between the roughness of the bales and the sleek exterior of the cling-film sheathing disturbs the normal architectural categories, uniting the slick with the hairy and the fetishised with the repressed.

The Duvet A cloth covering upholsters the office like a chair, reuniting the domestic artefact with the place of work. Puckered and buttoned, the external and internal are elided. Non-stick cloth. Silicone implanted fibres. Behind its apparent fluidity and weightlessness, the solid walls of the office resist the vibration of the trains passing by.

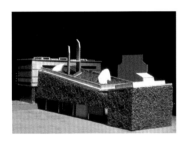

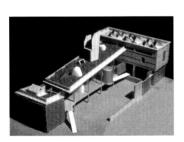

FROM ABOVE: View of model showing building in context; view of model with strawbale wall; view of model

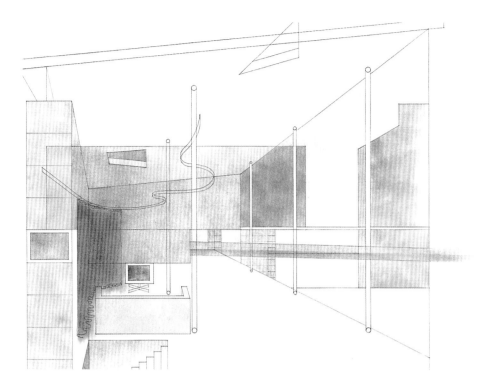

Story 3. Watching the World Go By

We are already living in the house we have yet to build. Constructed only through drawings, space and events compacted in our head. Straight ahead a television, that old 'window to the world'. But the velvet curtain is pulled back, so attention is distracted, views shifted. To the left, a housing estate caught in the deep reveal; he's doing his hair again, silhouetted against bobbly glass. To the right, picture windows picture the street; the new milkman looking for a doorstep. Ahead the office is suspended, waiting. Escape its presence upwards, through the rooflight and join the passing plane on its way to holiday romance. And through it all a train passes. It is the 10.05, the Edinburgh one.

Story 4. Scaling the Library

Stack of books. Worry about how to order them. Chronologically? Oldest at the bottom, like archaeology? Alphabetically? But Zola is a favourite and too long a climb. Thematically? But what is to be at the top, floating us heavenward, books of dreams or books of thoughts?

Start to climb, past the rude green lump, lights caught in its rough surface. The window salesman is in there, panicking at the waterless loo, confronting his own shit. Up past the balcony, cello waiting to learn to play. On up perforated stairs, criss-crossing between work and play. Through the roof, head level with the meadow, scorched in the sun. Room at the top still looks funny, leaning towards the trains. We have the timetables up there, a little joke. And at night, the roof draws back and we lie on the single bed, starwards.

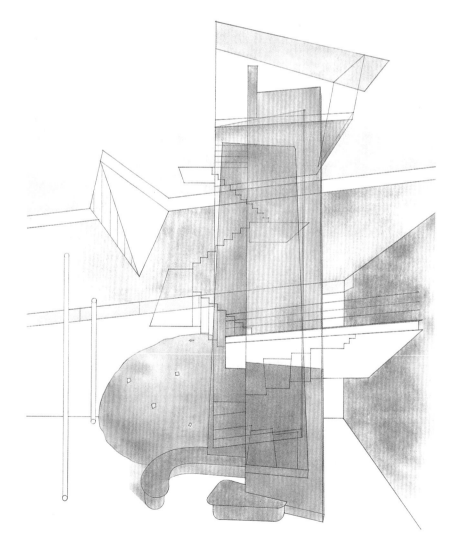

Scaling the library

PHILLIP HALL-PATCH
BREAKING THE VEIL

Designs which focus on notions of the everyday often begin by re-examining objects which are often taken for granted – those physical elements of our environment which are so part of our lives that we no longer seem to recognise or question them at a conscious level. But what of those processes which are hidden from view? Can these be revealed, and if so what part can they play in creating an architecture of the everyday? Central to these concerns are notions of technology, or more particularly, of technological systems which serve to create a veil to the reading of architecture.

This notion of the architectural veil operates on a number of levels each serving to suppress the sensual possibilities of architecture – a material architecture of engagement and experience. In this context, the overriding concern must be that of time and or/our ability to place materials and processes of construction within a time-frame: to read a building as one might read a palimpsest where the memory of previous constructions and embodiments (although indistinct) have left their trace; traces which the weathering effects of time itself may be allowed to magnify or conceal, but which may never be erased. By concealing material processes and presenting a mask of an idealised static state (or simply astounding with wizardry), the veil of technological determinism often becomes literal to the extent that it prevents or inhibits participation by the user in creating a personal sense of place.

Conventional technological systems are predominantly based upon the linear flow of energy and materials. Simply described, products are produced from raw materials (from supposedly infinite supplies), and when discarded are removed from sight to waste dumps and landfills; both the sourcing and the end result of our modern lifestyle is therefore removed from view. This kind of linear, or 'high' technology, cannot be extricated from the pervading influence of capitalism, an essential act of which is the exploitation of nature. It is commonly acknowledged that the seemingly limitless possibilities of the combination of science and technique, when combined with commercial pressures, lead to the ever-increasing obsolescence of technological gadgets. It is in the drive to constantly replace existing artefacts with the new and the better that any cultural significance is lost, thereby reducing us to the production of banal disposable products that have permeated every corner of our daily lives and which litter our environment.

Our basic social and functional interactions have come to be altered or defined by a complex system of intervening technologies which we do not understand and which cannot be seen. Modern technological developments have tended towards increasing miniaturisation, culminating in the development of 'nano-technology' (engineering and design at the atomic scale). Our ability to see, comprehend and understand such technologies is reduced. 'Alienation' is the term often used to describe this loss of unity between man and his environment, whilst notions of

ecology, in all its various guises, attempt to re-establish this missing link. The ecological argument makes the bold and somewhat scandalous suggestion that we might not need or even want many of the supposed benefits of many new technologies, and that the increasing need is to be able to differentiate between those which are benign and those which are destructive; to bring into our control and comprehension those techniques of the modern world that can be used for our own good. As technological innovation continues to breach the limits of physical possibilities, so we become ever more aware of the increasing existence of other environmental limits that we had previously not recognised. The irony is that it may be precisely the recognition of such limits that could hold the key for a new sensibility in what Manzini refers to as the 'ethic of the artificial'.[1]

Over the years the ecological movement has sustained a critique of capitalism and its associated means and tools of production (its exploitation of natural resources). But this does not imply a return to originary forms of nature. Perhaps the ecological movement's greatest contribution may be the expansion of traditional notions of 'nature' as a cultural construct. This is embodied in the move from the perception and objectification of passive *objects*, to a more active engagement with often imperceptible *systems of relationships*. Such a view asks us to question the extent to which meaning forms part of the environment or whether it is in the mind of the observer. 'Is a solid waste landfill *inherently* ugly because of some intrinsic pattern or characteristic independent of human experience, or does it trigger a complex set of culturally generated feelings and beliefs about human generated waste?'[2] If we can come to accept nature as a cultural construct then our culturally determined perceptions may be radically altered. The ecological movement therefore does not, and should not, imply a return to some pre-industrial past but rather a movement towards a more critical future.

Accepting also that technological systems carry implicit social systems (which alter the balance of power and authority in ways which we do not understand or choose to ignore), we may then also be able to consider the possibility of a technology encapsulated in an environmental and sustainable design ethic – one which includes the wider material and immaterial landscape. 'Intermediate Technology' (to use the correct technical term), is based on the notion of *appropriateness* of use and its *transparency*, in as much as the function and construction of any object or system can be understood and comprehended at any level. The principles of cyclical flows are inherent to this system, where re-use and appropriation become essential elements in the closing of resource loops.[3] Approaching design in this way may open up possibilities for an architecture not only rich in its physical and sensual properties, but one also potentially liberating in social and cultural terms.

It is therefore essential for any activity of design to recognise

Tadashi Kawamata, Relocation, *installation at Annely Juda Fine Art, London, 8 Aug-13 Sept 1997*

Mike Reynolds, Earthship, Taos,
New Mexico

Elemer Zalotay, House in Ziegelried,
Switzerland

Elemer Zalotay, House in Ziegelried,
Switzerland

the relation of the built object (or environment) to the complex interactions and webs of which it forms part. The present industrial age tends to focus on 'products' frozen in time, whilst the ecological perspective suggests that all that exists is process and that all objects exist as points within the continuum of change. This, then, is one of the fundamental properties of sustainability which cannot be removed from conceptions of time needed for such flows and cycles of connection to occur. By accepting time as an essential ingredient of nature, the temporal preoccupation can be used as an expression of natural processes of growth, change and flux by which a new aesthetic may evolve. Such an approach not only implies a new aesthetic, but also a new value system 'that attributes worth to materials and products that in some way are able to embody vestiges of their earlier existences'.[4] Through making connections to previous embodiments (as well as making these connections visible), we may begin to re-create a sense of meaning in the objects and artifacts that make up our environment. This then is the new sensuality of experience to which I have referred.

If working within a cyclical system implies moving from the veiled process of quantity production to the more transparent and qualitative nature of *re*-production (of working with materials that are regarded as part of a value-system with a history of their own), then the designer's role must be to make such processes visible. The implications of such an approach to architecture are profound – the development of processes of design which are never final and complete, but which grow and change in a way which one could say is truly responsive. Beyond this are the liberating effects of such *open* design which allow us at least the opportunity to reconnect to time and place as well as the possibility of repositioning ourselves within nature's systems. As Thayer points out, '"Place" is not only a sense of physical intimacy and locational uniqueness, it is also a sense of *connectedness* – a physical relationship to other places in a contextual web or matrix.'[5]

An architecture of this nature would be one which both creates form, and through the interaction of its maker, allows form to be created. A way of building which will make the process of construction, the passage of time and intangible qualities visible; giving expression to the use and the users. A dynamic architecture containing spontaneity and structural variety.

An example of precisely this kind of variety can be found in the 'Earthships' of New Mexico, where Mike Reynolds devised a number of methods for the transformation of urban waste into structural building materials. Reynolds provided simple step-by-step instructions which could be replicated with the simplest of tools, to provide shelter for a transient population in the most inhospitable of environments. Worn car tires can be rammed with earth to form circular 'bricks', whilst aluminium cans, when mortared together, have been used to create curved walls and even domed ceilings. Reynolds has an appropriately optimistic view of waste materials as both literal and metaphoric building blocks providing solutions to other problems – housing, energy and employment. He states that we have inadvertently been 'stockpiling ideal building materials for the future', whilst regarding tire dumps as 'potential communities, towns, and even cities of Earthships'.[6]

Importantly, although Reynolds makes suggestions as to the potential use and assembly of such 'found materials as bricks', the ultimate form is left to the discretion and personal creativity of the builder as *bricoleur*.

For architecture, the act of bricolage is to advocate more than simply the re-use or salvage of building materials, but the ability to reclaim materials from any source (cut-off's or waste) to fulfil a number of tasks in unexpected and unconventional ways, whilst actively participating in the process or act of making. Reynold's architecture (or more appropriately, the architecture Reynolds has initiated) goes beyond simply notions of 'self-build'; this is moreover an architecture speculating as to the possibilities 'of constructing as opposed to construction, of a dynamic state of "becoming" in preference to a static state of "being".'[7]

Reynolds' approach reiterates the idea of circular systems, or regenerative practices of design, providing at any one moment in time a restricted palate or set of finite materials. This supports Levi-Strauss' suggestion that there exists an *other* system of scientific thought; one based on concrete realities, where one's 'instrumental set' of tools (mental and creative processes) is constrained by those available materials.[8] As the instrumental set is limited, the actual potential (or necessity) for invention becomes greater, resulting in a broadened horizon of possibilities. Strauss defines the bricoleur as using such a closed set of finite materials, as opposed to the project of the engineer which presupposes that there are as many sets of tools and raw materials as there are projects (a classically linear system of technological thinking).

The 'bricoleur' is adept at performing a large number of diverse tasks; but unlike the engineer, he does not subordinate each of them to the availability of raw materials and

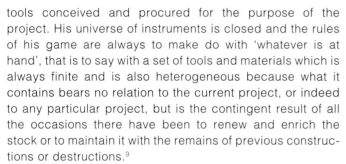

Shigeru Ban, Paper Log houses in Shinminatogawa Park, Kobe, Japan

Interior of Paper Log house

tools conceived and procured for the purpose of the project. His universe of instruments is closed and the rules of his game are always to make do with 'whatever is at hand', that is to say with a set of tools and materials which is always finite and is also heterogeneous because what it contains bears no relation to the current project, or indeed to any particular project, but is the contingent result of all the occasions there have been to renew and enrich the stock or to maintain it with the remains of previous constructions or destructions.[9]

The artist Tadashi Kawamata works in precisely such a manner using a restricted set of given materials and inventing a methodology and vocabulary of form specific to every project and responsive to every space. Working with architectural and often domestic fragments, the effects of his spaces are both surprising and astonishingly beautiful. As I have attempted to illustrate, with this kind of (for want of a better term) 'bricoloric'[10] activity the final scheme is never drawn as a finite conception, but develops as construction proceeds; spaces being allowed to grow and develop over time, out of the quality of the available material.

On a larger scale, Elemer Zalotay has built an experimental home in Ziegelried, Switzerland, where through engaging with a limited set of 'waste' materials, he attempted to develop a panel system that could be used as a series of modular units. Although more involved in scope and execution, a similar working method to that of Kawamata can be detected, even if the final results are markedly different. Similarities exist only on the level of invention and complexity.

The social and economic implications of such a mode of design, in its encouragement to self-help (and self-thought), are far reaching and may be seen by society as threatening to established orders and codes of behaviour. The transgression of

one such order is that of what traditionally constitutes professionalism, for, as I hope my illustrations have shown, it is not necessarily innate capability, exclusive access to knowledge or the capacity to master skills that determines the social distinctions between professional and non-professional designers, but qualities such as invention and imagination when working with a limited set of literal and metaphoric tools.

Finally, Shigeru Ban's 'Cardboard City', emergency housing built in response to the Kobe earthquake of 1995, was developed using recycled paper tubes (or columns) supported off damp ground on plastic beer crates, the structures coming to be known as 'Paper Log Houses'. These are now being developed as semi-permanent housing for refugees in Nairobi. What is of interest here is the way in which this kind of regenerative design seems to be more forgiving to expressions of domesticity than much modern design which attempts to veil or suppress our day-to-day actions and feelings behind pristine, impenetrable surfaces.

However, the danger exists of aestheticising material effects in the search for a new style or fetish which may itself become obsolete when exposed to the vagaries of fashion and taste. An 'aesthetic of recycling' would be in fact just as insidious and veiling as the aesthetic of hi-technology. To avoid this danger we have to move beyond the surface and redeploy the processes that go towards the making of any artifact.

Whilst drawing on its principles, what I am proposing is a more critical alternative to conventional ecology, one which holds many implications for architecture of both a material and social nature. My argument has been that through breaking the veil of normative technological systems and accepting cyclical modes of engagement and *re-production*, we may discover new possibilities for material and cultural transformations, and in so doing begin to make an architecture of long-term significance.

Notes

1 Ezio Manzini, 'Prometheus of the Everyday: The Ecology of the Artificial and the Designer's Responsibility', in R Buchanan, and V Margolin (eds), *Discovering Design: Explorations in Design Studies*, University of Chicago Press (Chicago), 1995, p228.

2 Robert L Thayer, *Gray World, Green Heart: Technology, Nature, and the Sustainable Landscape*, John Wiley & Sons (New York), 1994, p104.

3 For an in-depth appraisal of 'linear' versus 'cyclical' technological systems, see: John Tillman Lyle, *Regenerative Design for Sustainable Development*, John Wiley & Sons (New York), 1992.

4 Manzini, 'Prometheus of the Everyday', op cit, p236.

5 Thayer, *Gray World, Green Heart*, op cit, p200.

6 Epilogue in Michael Reynolds, *Earthship*, vol 1: *How to Build Your Own*, Solar Survival Press (Taos, New Mexico), 1990.

7 Mike Kohn, 'Building a Bricolage: An Architecture of Improvisation, Second-Handedness, Salvage and Re-use', unpublished diploma thesis, University College London, 1997, p1.

8 Claude Levi-Strauss, *The Savage Mind*, Weidenfeld and Nicolson (London), 1966, pp17-18.

9 Ibid.

10 Kohn suggests 'bricoloric' as an adjective pertaining to the practice of 'bricolage'. Kohn, 'Building a Bricolage', op cit, p5.

MICHAEL MARRIOTT
GUARANTEED CAST IRON

Working primarily as a furniture/product designer my concerns with the everyday are often related to the simple and familiar utilitarian objects which surround us. I am interested in playing with familiar or everyday iconography as a means of intriguing viewers and encouraging them to enjoy modern objects. I feel this requires creating objects that are not just about gratuitous, egotistical or fashion-led form making, but that have real ideas behind their forms. Some of these objects can become accessible through the cunning appropriation of familiar elements which can then act as a canvas on which to lay fresh ideas.

It seems to me that many of the text book examples of 'Modernism' are more about a kind of 'reductionism' and therefore become only 'modernist style', whilst many of the more unassuming, everyday, utilitarian objects that surround us are actually much truer to modernist philosophy. As well as being genuinely more 'modern', these familiar everyday objects tend to be less brutal, more honest and more human than the 'modernist styled', which can deteriorate too easily into just an assembly of soulless geometrical parts.

When designing an object I have sometimes found it pertinent to appropriate familiar elements (whether they are forms, materials, processes or characteristics). Whilst considering the design of a candlestick, I decided that cast iron could provide a relevant and interesting combination of material and process. Because of its heavy industrial nature it is usually relegated to beneath the bodywork of vehicles or other such utilitarian uses, and is consequently seen as being grubby and therefore of low

L to R: Cast Iron Candlesticks, 1996; utilitarian lump of cast iron

value. Whilst analysing the material and looking to exploit its intrinsic characteristics, I established that, as well as coming with its own useful and reassuring weight, it also had very satisfying tactile qualities when sand-cast. Another advantage of using cast iron was that there was already a large pre-existing genre of objects from which to draw for familiar traits and knowledge. Due to the manufacturing process involved, this group of objects often has a wonderfully rich vocabulary of form and also a willing capacity for incorporated text, which happily allows for added ingredients.

Using cast iron in the design of a small table-top product such as a candlestick brings to light its quiet beauty by moving it into the domestic landscape, but through the back door. The form of the finished object is informed not only by the existing genre and the process, but also by pure function and quiet wit. The incorporated text, 'Guaranteed Cast Iron', is part of a generic typology, but it is also stating very obviously what the object is manufactured from, despite its gold colour. On the underside of the object there is a quality control sticker which states, 'This Product Comes with a Cast Iron Guarantee'. As well as corresponding with its type, the stove enamelled gold finish 'softens' the industrial nature of the material and is a reference to the ubiquitous polished brass candlestick.

It could be argued that cast aluminium would be a more sensible alternative for this product – it could be much cheaper to process. But I feel it would seem too insubstantial and lightweight, and as a raw material, iron is cheaper, less destructive to mine from the earth and, like all the best modern materials, bio-degradable.

LEFT TO RIGHT: Iron casting; Cast Iron Candlesticks, 1996, underside; Cast Iron Candlesticks, 1996, with packaging

NÍALL MCLAUGHLIN

SHACK
Foxhall, Northamptonshire

Water modulates light. Gina is a photographer who makes fragile still-life images. I
showed her my picture of objects
arranged at different depths in a boghole
and she began to imagine projects where
a pond surface, teeming with life, is
captured on film. Water would be used to
alter the depth of field and to veil the light.
We discussed the possibility of oxygenat-
ing water in an old pond, to attract dragon-
flies. The pond, which stands between her
garden and open farmland, was stagnant
and lost in a tangle of briar. We began to
open up the site, renovating it using fish,
water plants and filtration. (**1**)

1

2

The farmland had been used as a US
reconnaissance base during the Second
World War. Flights of B-24 black 'carpet-
bagger' bombers flew clandestine mis-
sions from the adjacent woods, bringing
supplies to the resistance in Holland,
Norway and France. After the war the site
was developed as a nuclear missile base
and was abandoned in the mid-1960s.
The land is now littered with the debris of
military hardware. An entire dismantled
bomber is buried close to the pond. (**2**)

We developed a design by comparing
the camera lens hovering over the water,
capturing images of insects, to the
reconnaissance flights from the base,
bringing back images from remote landscapes. Susan Sontag compares the
photographer to a hunter:

3

> Still, there is something predatory in
> the act of taking a picture . . . Guns
> have metamorphosised into cameras
> in this earnest comedy, the ecology
> safari, because nature has ceased to
> be what it has always been – what
> we need protection from. Now nature
> tamed, endangered, mortal – needs
> to be protected from people. When
> we are afraid we shoot. But when we
> are nostalgic, we take pictures. (**3**)

This early collage was intended to fix an
image of the building before it was
analysed as an architectural proposition.
It is a dark wing-like form at the edge of
the pond. As we were making the drawing, Simon Storey called by the office on

8

business. He liked the image and the story of the site. His father had been a Spitfire pilot flying reconnaissance during the last war. We discussed ways in which the building might be made using very simple materials. Simon agreed to build it for £15,000 on the condition that no construction drawings were produced. (**4**)

Models and photographs of models were used to design, explain and construct this small building. Gina is not happy interpreting architectural drawings, but loves to be drawn along by photographs, reinventing the design through them. Simon knows that the model allows him to read the specification more creatively, opening up a gap between the instruction and its execution. The model allows me to invent a building which changes constantly as you move through and around it. These rough little objects opened out the development process, making it available to all of the participants. (**5**)

The brief expanded as it encountered family democracy. Gina's partner, Geof, wanted a sauna and the children wanted a bed to make the shack a retreat from the house. When a client changes or develops the programme during the design it is initially frustrating for the architect who is formulating an order out of the existing programme. It is also the moment when the project is most alive, laid open to inventive change. The client's particular life is the most powerful engine of development for an architect who, for good reasons, is absorbed in his own aesthetic discourse. (**6**)

The structure is examined in this x-ray image. The wing members are surmounted by perforated metal canopies. Our engineer, Tony Hayes, saw the structural design as stopping the building from floating or flying away, rather than keeping it standing up. A concrete raft and rendered block walls hold the space on the edge of the water. The roof is of

plywood, fibreglass, polycarbonate and metal. The structure is allowed to flap, flex and deflect in the very strong winds which buffet the site. It is tethered by slender steel rods. (**7**)

The building recalls Anselm Kiefer's paintings of the scorched earth of Germany after the war. It is a dark wing-like form hovering over the arable land and marks the boundary of the farm and the garden. The underside of the wing is a luminous cavity which arches over the water, capturing light in its folds. (**8**)

The side of the building which faces the house was developed as a facade. A thick wall acts like an armature, supporting the roof, the lantern, the canopies and the sauna structure. Small openings, set into the wall, admit light which is used in the photographic process. At the lowest point in the wall, tucked under the wing, is a tiny entrance door accessed by stepping stones on the pond. (**9**)

The lantern appeared in an early

9

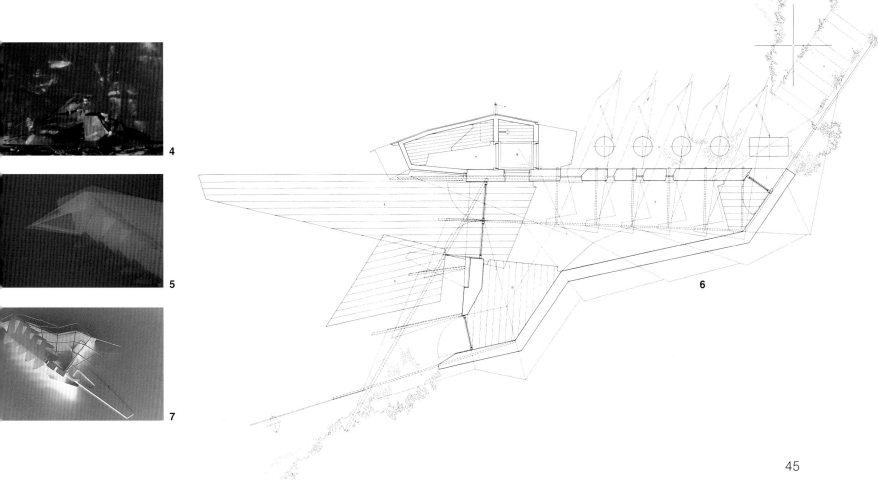

4

5

7

6

45

collage and has remained with the project despite having no vocation in relation to the programme. Construction was suspended for months while I made hundreds of models trying to integrate it into the building. It has been variously interpreted as an eye or a head or a cockpit. As I remember it first, it was something gorgeous set against the swathe of the wing, a brooch to hold the dark cloak in place. (**10**)

10

Alan Wharburton made the canopies from galvanised perforated metal. They are designed like petals to flex and lap over each other. Slender tie rods hold them down and maintain a slight inbuilt bow in the flat sheet. The rods are secured underwater. The freckled pattern of light cast by the canopies is printed onto the polycarbonate baffles below. (**11**)

11

The blind wall is a register for collected light. Fantastic multiple exposures overlap on this surface as brightness comes, either direct from the sky, filtered and made to flicker by trees or wavering as it reflects back off the water. The image of each aperture is printed twice, once by direct and once by reflected light. The light moves at different speeds depending on what has modulated it; water, clouds, branches, canopies, baffles. Occasionally, a slender amber shaft tracks across the composition, sneaking through from the high lantern. (**12**)

12

Each window acts as a stage for the photographic process. Objects are collected and held in the light. They are allowed to dry, bloom or go off. They are sifted and sorted in the small windows. The large square opening is set at eye level so that compositions can be photographed in it.

13

Gina and Geof have softened the bleached purity of the interior with rugs and kilims. It is always a surprise to see your building occupied. Often it changes the way in which you understand it. I had a clear, but not articulated, preconception of the architectural pedigree of my design. As soon as I saw the shag rug I realised, 'Oh God! It's Bruce Goff!' (**13**)

Numbers in brackets refer to images.

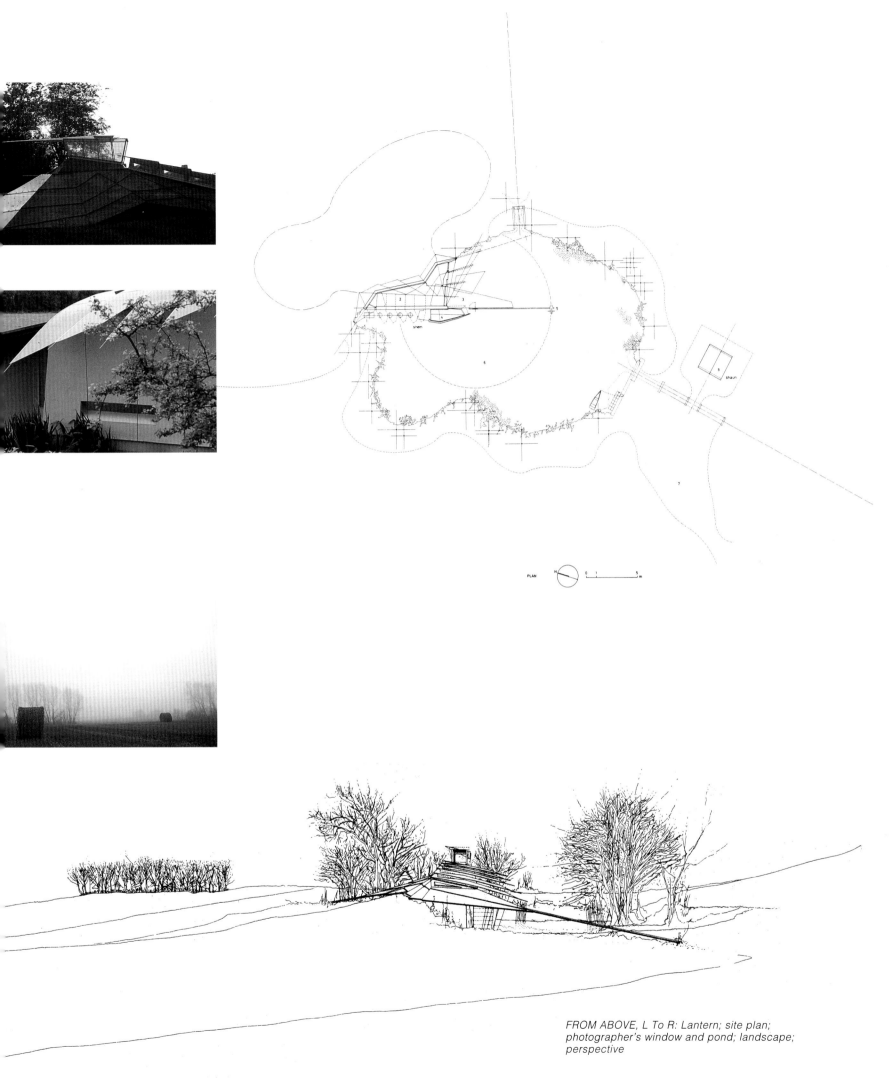

*FROM ABOVE, L To R: Lantern; site plan;
photographer's window and pond; landscape;
perspective*

BEN KELLY DESIGN

INTERIORS 'R' US

Ben Kelly interviewed by Sarah Wigglesworth

We sit at a large table in Ben Kelly Design's first-floor office, in an area separated from the rest of the space by Dexion shelving units. This must be the meeting room but the table top is strewn with piles of papers, memos, faxes: things to do, things in progress. To the left and right of us lie hundreds of samples of different materials. They are stacked around the room on almost every available surface – floor, chimney mantle, shelving units, tabletop, window sill. There are slates, plastics, glass blocks, sections of timber, metals, sharing space with the cardboard box files which are dedicated to each job. Were it not for the detritus of office life, the atmosphere would be almost frugal.

The window overlooks Borough market, now quiet. Every so often an overhead train pulls by or sits momentarily stationary on the brick arches above our heads, waiting for the signal to change. Eventually it clatters on its way to south London. Despite this there is an air of concentration and industry. People come and go; the phone rings. This is a working office. No pretensions, no frills, beautiful hand-drawn drawings placed on the boards. It strikes me that Ben Kelly Design's office is like their work: it respects what is given, it doesn't muck about with it. There is meticulous attention to detail, to sourcing the right product, to getting the sensation of the real thing, to feeling the effect of a colour in the flesh. The palette is fashionable, but it isn't flash.

Ben Kelly Design's work is already well known; Kelly is becoming something of an establishment figure. He was among a number of the brightest young talent recently invited to no 10 Downing Street, honoured with several prestigious prizes and, following the commission for the children's gallery at the Science Museum, his firm is now designing the new offices for the Design Council in Covent Garden. 'Increasingly for Ben Kelly Design, our ambitions lie in dealing with the public and improving the public's lot. This implies working in public spaces – the shop, the High Street, the pavement. Up to a couple of years ago the office was operating on the periphery.' Nowadays Kelly is more interested in meeting men in suits 'because that is where the power is'. It is a matter of the simplest route to reaching a wider audience: 'The High Street is a mess and the stranglehold of the big companies needs breaking down. It needs some integrity, some intellectual rigour.' Ben Kelly Design is poised to target the mainstream; as he says, 'Marks & Spencer's would be a great commission'.

Ben Kelly Design is no stranger to the High Street. The firm's first job was for the Howie store in Covent Garden, in 1977. Kelly describes his design as an attempt to make the interior an object in its own right, shifting the convention that privileged the object over its setting. In the sense that this meant retail design became a brand product – like any product – it could then be marketed in its own right. It is a far cry from M&S, where the shop interior plays a conventional role as neutral backdrop to its merchandise and seeks to unify its image under a blandness which challenges the public as little as possible. In the Howie store, the branding was the result of unlikely juxtapositions of elements and the free play of materials and colour from different periods and sources, which relocates them in a contemporary context: 'I retain in the original what works and what is beautiful as well as certain memories of the past, whether as salvaged fragments of the building, references to its former use or spatial echoes.' The trick Ben Kelly Design used was to take ordinary materials and objects and recombine them in ways which make them extraordinary. It was to become a successful formula in subsequent designs which have included the Hacienda Club, the American Retro Store, Dry 201 and Bar 10.

Ben Kelly Design's work has always been associated with the fashionable, avant-garde end of the High Street. By definition, this is a world which has a limited life, heavily conscious of its age. It seeks out the unexpected, the strange and the exciting. Its appeal is to the discerning, the style conscious and the hip. Drawing on the public realm as one of its inspirations, it acknowledges it as a scene in which incongruous events come together and chance encounters take place. There is fun, temporariness, movement, colour. Surroundings are acknowledged as possessing a history and a life of their own – just like the city – which can never be completely controlled or erased. Indeed, the presence of this 'other' gives

OPPOSITE: Produktion Offices, London, 1995; FROM ABOVE: DRY 201, Manchester, 1989; the Hacienda Club, Manchester, 1982

FROM ABOVE: National Museum of Science and Industry, London, 1995, basement; Produktion Offices, London, 1995

something to kick against, to play with, to reinvent, rejuvenate.

In the Hacienda, which had formerly been a yachting showroom, the idea of the street literally enters the interior. The cleared void of the volume, with its naked structure, rasping colours, bold graphics and existing infrastructure makes reference to the exterior world. The raw concrete columns were painted using striped black-and-colour, like a multi-storey car park. As with the street, it is consciously understated, its apparent 'ordinariness' belying the effort that contributes to its success. In a commercial sleight of hand, the same branding was extended to all parts of the Factory Records stable (club, graphics, record label, offices).

Similar ideas re-emerge in the project for the Science Museum. Here, a huge underground space was to accommodate up to 2,000 school kids each day of the week. The children were to use the space as an orientation room, a place to hear talks, a place of fun, a picnic area and a shop. Kelly describes the key marker in his relationship with the client as the moment when the client said he envisaged the design as 'a Hacienda for kids'. Ben Kelly Design's response was once again to clear the basement of clutter and expose the essential structural elements – concrete columns, floors and beams – of the interior. Into this he inserted brightly coloured elements in plastics, metal, lino – common, inexpensive materials but not often used in combination like this. Raw but playful, the design revels in addressing the pragmatic demands of thousands of children rather than shrinking from them. In the redeployment of ordinary, everyday materials and forms Ben Kelly Design creates an architecture which is genuinely engaging, far removed from the remote aesthetics of high architectural culture. This is a paradigm shift in what constitutes architecture.

In all these commissions, the unifying theme is one where the robust, ordinary features of the street, qualities not normally associated with high design, are celebrated in their own right. What is usually background is foregrounded and becomes its own aesthetic. In addition, it asks us to address the things we overlook because we take them for granted, acting as a means of engagement with habitual, commonplace uses and objects. By this definition alone Ben Kelly Design's work would qualify as 'everyday'.

Ben Kelly Design's recent work has involved designing office interiors, the setting in which many of us spend our waking hours. Characteristic themes emerge: a keen interest in practical matters, use of colour, interest provided by limits to views and semi-transparency, a sampling of elements from eclectic sources. Above all, one or two interesting textures and materials that seem out of place at first sight. In the Produktion offices it is the use of Douglas fir, a coarse-patterned, varied timber, which looks as sophisticated as shuttering ply. Curiously, Kelly first saw it used by Donald Judd, and cites it as an example of one source for the crossover into the 'art interior' he said he wanted to produce during his interview for a place at the Royal College of Art. Clearly, Kelly does not view his work as everyday.

The interior embodies the everyday more comprehensively than architecture. It is, almost literally, the backdrop to people's daily lives, the reality behind the soap set. The interior is less totalising, less monumental than architecture, and doesn't shirk the question of taste, which architecture tries to avoid. Frequently interiors are fantasies (which architecture is rarely explicit about), and they are easily changed when they wear out, which is, by definition, also frequently. Luckily, they are usually less ambitious than architecture (it can involve choosing just a single object), and therefore cheap(er). Interiors are ubiquitous but deliberate. We may not all own bricks and mortar, but most of us buy furniture, wallpaper, cutlery, paint, lights; we choose upholstery, carpets and kitchen equipment. These things 'R' us.

Interiors are inclusive, not exclusive. Architecture, hung up on its own dignity and obsessed with its own immortality, adheres to the rules, while interiors break them. Interiors operate tactically on the fabric of architecture, poaching it, appropriating it and using its space and surfaces to unexpected ends. The interesting things happen in the unpoliced places because these are the areas that cannot be controlled – let alone predicted – by the designer. Ben Kelly Design's work is important because their interiors seem to recognise this. They acknowledge that the fun happens when odd things come together, and it is significant that this is also the way in which buildings are used in everyday life. In this sense Ben Kelly Design is ahead of the game. As they move increasingly onto the same stage as architecture and are in a position to command the mainstream, all architects should take note.

National Museum of Science and Industry, London, 1995, basement

ÅSMUND THORKILDSEN
TURNING THE COMMONPLACE, SURE...
A Poetic Appreciation of Jessica Stockholder's Art

... the leaves of the forest turned, one by one, to crimson and to gold, but never broke off ...
They glow, the humblest of them, to the imagination ...
Henry James, The American Scene, *1907*

In Untitled, *1979, he uses scraps of newsprint which have yellowed. On one clipping, the word white is printed in black ink on paper which has 'turned' from white to yellow.*
William S Wilson on Jasper Johns, 1992

Artists have done it for centuries – turned the ordinary into something rich and strange. They imitate nature in this. Language, pictures, art work make this happen. As Shakespeare wrote *The Tempest* he saw the eyes of the drowned sailor undergo a sea change. They became pearls. And it happens again, every year when the New England Fall – or autumn as the expatriate Henry James called it – turns the green leaves into a flaming symphony in yellows, oranges and reds. In fairy tales frogs turn into princes. In art nothing is exactly what meets the innocent eye. Faces are eyes that blush as they turn.

Henry James likened the New England scenes he so acutely observed to paintings. It is hard to see landscape as raw experience. Even the vagueness of the impression is drenched in a golden haze – the vagueness is drenched in two words – *golden haze*. Once consciousness works, the fluctuating, ephemeral vagueness of what is in front of him is apprehended by an act of the mind in perception. James – like American artists succeeding him – uses an art that reconciles him with the arbitrary. Once art has entered, the clouds read as feathery brush strokes and the flicker of light and shade reads as impressionism. James is true to his times and sees the scenery of the New England coast line in the likeness of a Japanese colour print.

The American Scene is the title of Henry James' travel book written following the first visit to his native shores after a quarter of a century abroad. The meeting with the land and landscapes of his childhood and youth is one of mixed blessings. His complicated and endlessly reworked experience of the changed and lingering environment turns his mind in a way that expresses itself in the most embroidered and convoluted prose of his late style. Nothing is experienced at all unless as a stream of multilayered impressions, reflections and musings. What promises to be a simple, immediate and unmediated sight or view soon turns into artful and meandering sequences of language. He wills the American scene into literature.

James could not quite reconcile himself with the blankness and grimness of the American commonplace. He tries, but he is taken in by his memory and art – he had fled the US in order to take part in the sophisticated airs of Europe. The American common presented itself as a series of sames. Extremes of life were missing in the continuous spread of elm lined streets, and rows of white painted houses. James was not a man for the commonplace. But not quite, the lack of distinctions in the vagueness and overall first impression is turned into art by the author's active experience when he sees, remembers, arranges and brings together the analysed parts of what first struck him as uneventful and plain.

James' mind craved for the extremes that made his life interesting and satisfied his restlessness and curiosity. For him it was art that made the appreciation of distinctions possible. Reconciliation works by the infiltration of language. Metaphors make it possible to write down impressions of natural phenomena, ready-mades to the restless analyst. The scenes of New England are invested with the richness and congruity of his imagination resulting in the embroidered surfaces of the fully formulated contemplation.

It is perhaps strange to call on Henry James when it comes to an artist like Jessica Stockholder. Her art has none of the detached, aristocratic and sometimes condescending ways of the displaced brahmin. Hers is an art of the commonplace, yet it turns on the commonplace with art.

There is something alluring and seductive in Jessica Stockholder's installations. One is taken in by the unexpectedness of the obvious. The common objects she uses as building materials are woven into full-scale, three-dimensional installations that invite direct participation. One moves easily in them; they offer surprises, shifts, obstacles. They give the same sense of postponed pleasure as when one first learned how to skate, to swim or to ride a bike. The installations are built with ready-made objects used exactly like words in language. There is a pleasure resembling that of the language one was so eager to learn how to use. Her installations make visible the overlapping or turns of a visual and physical sequence, when one element is sharpened and fuses into something else. These shifts are transpositions of one practical thing into another, which turns into visual fact, into visual and cerebral meaning, into words, which are paramount in Stockholder's art. Stockholder's is an aesthetics of falling and coming up again. It descends and ascends. Hailstorm as well as firework.

As Henry James put it: 'every fact was convertible into fancy'. Stockholder overlaps nature with culture, bridges the gap between the house and its lot, its inside with the out of doors. The force of a coloured surface leaps into another area, marking the terrain, an energy that turns words to show the flip side of language. All this is quite obvious, like the obviousness of moving and resting the body, the sequence and workings of one's appetite and the gratification of eating. Stockholder turns common objects so that the audience is involved body and soul in the sight and the fanciful uttering of words that sometimes pop up from under the cover of an ordinary object.

Every art work is an entity. A Stockholder installation has its very specific mechanics involving the interrelation of parts, but

there is still a whole, a formulation in several parts that takes a given space or set of spaces as the given in which to make a statement, with and against that space's architecture. The question is how should one approach a large work of Stockholder's? Should one accept it as a vague, undifferentiated impression, overwhelming in its vastness? What concerns our appreciation of Jessica Stockholder's art is not James' desire for the vague, the fusion of elements in a golden glow. The turning point lies in his inability to formulate the immediacy and oneness of this first impression and desire in language. His language is sequential, full of bristling particulars, as in a Jessica Stockholder installation that makes meaning by turning from pink to red to orange to yellow to green to black to white, as when a green wall (backed by a dense mass of solid black) turns the facing wall to white (igniting the white of a huge mass of plastic wrapped hay bales).

In the Kunstnernes Hus installation it is physically impossible to see the whole installation in one view. One can sense and remember the huge mass, the sliding movements running through parts of the work, and the vast bulk of parts in the installation. The wholeness is one of art, the things Stockholder does to make the installation something other than a collection of materials. The wholeness lies in the contemplation of the sequence of the installation in contrast to the strict symmetry of the two large spaces it spans.

The same aesthetic dilemma is woven into James' writing. His Arcadia is a place where questions drop and vagueness reigns, and the various references to 'a harmonious golden haze', 'a mild September glow', 'a New Jersey condition' and 'the clear October blaze' are ways of saying this. But the quest is contrary to the writing. In the writing there are several deferrals, insertions, differences; the one impression, its afterthought, its other, its possible contrary is distinguished. The restless analyst is par-

ticular when it comes to the naming – singling out every possible distinguishing factor from the mass. The calm is interrupted with his afterthoughts; his vocabulary and memories infiltrate the harmonious sentiment and an immediate experience turns into a word play in which he is careful to insert a mention of the distinctions between the names of a state and a part of the country. In the passage on Arcadia James makes a piece of art criticism, which hardly is an arcadian enterprise. He writes: 'admirable art'.

The restless analyst seems to find the aesthetic value of his environment in the vague, either in his New England autumn or when musing over Mrs Millers' nightly walk on the lakefront at Vevey, Switzerland. Does this lingering feeling of ubiquitous vagueness entail that the aesthetic experience is unutterable, a mere – if full – fleeting impression, something that is not really there at all, something that withdraws as it approaches, a glimpse beyond the strictures and reach of the rules of language, not graspable in words, something one cannot quite – or at all – express? Henry James' art (language) belies this. The vague is carried forth, laid out as a picture to vision, articulated in highly literary sentences that are all but without expression. The expression of the vague is – just as the senses all but threaten to leave one at a loss – to dare to form an opinion, the spring of an assessment, that, when formulated in descriptive language, will put even the most precarious of observers to a fragile test, who, if he dons the temporary challenge, will be blessed with judgements, carefully measured by the tentative analyst, of a much belated, but not for that reason regrettable, taste.

Stockholder's work is neither idyllic nor quaint. The reality of heavy matter, of cumbersome obstacles, serves as a counterpoint to the featherlight flight of the imagined idealist. The dense mass of enormous volumes – residues spilled from the ordinary

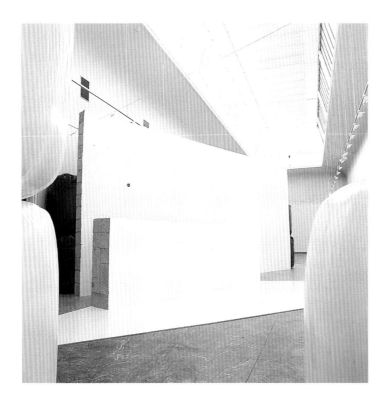

reservoir of things – turns to open spaces, brings light into the in-betweens that are energised by some glorious art, conventionally thought to emanate from what one could call the bulbous masses. Jessica Stockholder's constructions destroy the orderly simplicity of classical symmetric architecture. The installation is a huge footprint, stepping down on the unspoiled soil of the museum's floor. Curating a Stockholder installation is like working on a building site, fighting the hostilities of the environment. [Frank O'Hara wrote: 'Composition is a function of the sensibility; it is the personal statement of the insight which observation and insight afford. It is also an "agreement for cessation of hostilities" (*Concise Oxford Dictionary*) between oneself and nature.'] The sequence of the narrative, the sequence of the bowels, the sequence of a drift where gaze and eating are not one (William S Wilson on Simone Weil) sparks the high ride of thought and feeling, a Coney Island of the Mind (Ferlinghetti), a New York State of Mind, a New Jersey Condition, the soar and dredge of language taking us back to the thrills of the roller coaster (Lynne Tillman). All language is transgressive, whether verbal or visual, when it does the unheard of, showing its true colours and backsides. The movement isn't still, the shuttle moves to and fro, the sequences move by turns and shifts and screws. Flowers face the sun and move accordingly, trumpets turn into brightly coloured discs with the perfect rings of a bull's eye and a target, setting Léger and Johns *en rapport* with nature. There is some beginning, some end, or – to put it more precisely, somewhere to start and somewhere to end; the beguile is in between and up and down. The astonishment of the adventurous journey of being alive exposed to artful turns, on a swing, high up in a New Hampshire apple tree (TS Eliot). Transgression is in the transpositions, when one thing collects energies to shout out or shoot into something other. Transgression is not informal at all, it is anything but. Transgression is precise, sharp as a knife, and cruel as a scythe cutting the firebreak to bring forth the 'The moan of death' (William Everson). The huge stacks of Stockholder's hay bales are there for no reason at all, but for the scythe's rioting in the grass (Everson). Physical carriers are not lifted in dialectical transcendence (Hans Hofmann), but are bound tight together by the hot incandescent lightning that penetrates walls and makes the imagination slide in an installation that topples, falls and is put to rest. 'The word in the hand is the sound in the eye is the sight in the/listening ear. Listen, do you mind. Mind the solid pattern of all this soundless patter, collected together only in the writing.' (Robert Duncan)

Delmore Schwartz wrote a poem celebrating the beautiful American word 'sure'. Language works that way. Sometimes it turns on the expected, that is why language has sex appeal, it turns you on – sure. I am talking about 'the fun of pursuing the ensuing phrases' (Duncan). I am talking about installations that work after the measure of a sentence visualised like rows of uneven teeth (Duncan) or like the Manhattan sky line seen in the image of an old comb with missing teeth resting on its back (James); about 'The violence of a face cut open bleeding'. (Duncan)

Jessica Stockholder's work is rich, strange, dense, it covers over, hovers over; it pops with desire, lies under its yoke, bulges and kicks; it is fully unexpected and ordinary, amusing, wonderful and – very sensual.

Writing towards, in advance
SLAB OF SKINNED WATER, CUBED CHICKEN AND WHITE SAUCE

Piled high, tied high – yellow up close wrapped around the looking – road insulation dog down deep.
     Yellow green filled air, tense.

Blue grey
blue blue blue blue blue blue . . .
Bipolar. Tied through the building. A knot. Tied the knot, and so bringing detail to a wedding cake.
The forest lights up with vigor and sun. It is plastered to the walls. But its tendrils stretch out through hard concrete; through the room of moving bodies to grasp at the other end.
Lumps that sit unabashed as they are on the floor.

Floor covering – sanitized forest swamp woods.
     On the synthetic carpet and the wood grain linoleum. Through the prefab materials of building. Between them a haze of electric sparks so bright; they carry on. There is a party in the quiet moving. Over the swamp. That thick skin is showing through.

     One Two Black balcs, White. Display room veneer. Lagoons building past the show room.
     Snaking cake doilies.
     Lightness holding through the substantial unmoving grandeur.

     Inside space thumps where once it wasn't aloud.
     Tight, a thump hole hazed.

     Let's try again . . . Padding up the stairs. A little yellow carpet takes by surprise. Soft. There is a concept overlaid. A structure to the drawing that is visible from your perch in the hot air balloon hovering over the building.
     Down here, walking in gravity, legs like rubber; with blood, it is very slow.
     Big and plastic. Patterned. Left ore and right. The snow or the fire. But there is no ice to melt. Wiggling like a tadpole through the very shallow space between sheet plastic filled with light. Wet, lushness, mucous membranes.
     And so it all happened one day. Life begins and begins. It began. Rowing upstream. There are two banks to the river. From the middle each a picture makes. The river suspends and boats are caught between the two banks in the air. A cloud of turns, sight lines and neural connectors.

     As if from below, rupturing. No bones about it. This is not true; a falsehood.
     No bones about it. Wrapped, snuggled, fluffed about the bone that is not there. The slime on top slithers in bright day light; there is no dark cave from whence it came.
     The confusion, irrational, lapses in memory, joyous jumps over cliffs and gaps so wide. All there in the bright sun of the
 everyday.
     Those sacs, raised high on pedestals. Sacs of fluid bursting full.
     Against the raw plainness of the refrigerator white stepping stones.
     Sharp knife edge, flat against the cutting. Every so often. The news travels. And the flat minuscule gems of shininess pus up in the middle. Very slowly they make their mark.

     Ever so often. Left so often right. Smiling sunset smiling soften over wedding cake.

     The blue plush pile of the ragged carpet. And the thief took off roaring, chattering of trash can – metallic, thin, and brittle, down the steps. Gone into the night – out of sight. Rushing breathless into the thin golden viscous twilight that is his friend. Only it was up. The sea-saw never moved.

     Fluffed sunset roaring pale thin golden tubes. Tubes holding goo straight down the river. Lying flat against the stones and slabs of water squeezed, cubed wrapped like rubber. Golden light broken by cold blue sausages iced, laced, paired skin touching. If water slabs have skin.
     Slug slime trails in this garden would be like highways through trees. Incongruous paleness. Slab of skinned water, cubed chicken and white sauce.
     Skinned water winds its weightless way through air like a prism; all colors present. The dividing lines link boxes embraced, becoming only, single like yellow or red.
     The skin of this interview is a very thin line. The skin of this interior is a very thin Place pressured to bursting. Hard clear lines followed by dribbling, fluid chaos, languid action. Fruitiness abounds in this jungle, forever sprouting green shoots towards the sun. The thin membrane like saranwrap shows all.

     Walking from the studio to the house. My package of writings under arm. The season just changed. So many hours of inactivity. These words make bridges, stories in the air, on this page, tied to thoughts of stuff, matter, material in space, not the body. These words, one with actors peopling the landscape.
                                      Jessica Stockholder, Oslo, August 1997

KATHARINA LEDERSTEGER-GOODFRIEND

CHALLENGING PARADIGMS

Three Variations on Housing the Homeless in Los Angeles

Homelessness is certainly not a new problem, but the 1996 Welfare Reform Bill has renewed interest in the discussion of homelessness in the United States.[1] Many fear that the urban poor could be caught in a job crisis, adding further to the numbers of homeless people that have steadily increased since the economic decline of the 1970s.

This situation poses a particular problem for Los Angeles, which became the homeless capital of the United States during the 1980s. Economic restructuring in the region exclusively increased demand for low-skilled labour. Lower wages without pension and health benefits meant that more working people were living in poverty; simultaneously, welfare programs were downsized and affordable housing units were demolished and replaced by upmarket rentals and condominiums.[2]

Even as the boom of the later 1980s spawned a renewed interest in the development and preservation of cities, it did nothing to ameliorate the situation of the urban poor. In Los Angeles, successful regeneration projects such as the Third Street Promenade and Old Town Pasadena were hailed as signs of a new sense of urbanity, but coincided with overcrowding in low-income neighbourhoods as people doubled up or moved into illegal garden and garage units. Unsurprisingly, the growing numbers of homeless people sleeping on sidewalks, beaches, and public parks did not fit the new Disneyfied image of the city. Even in more liberal areas of Los Angeles, home-owner associations worried more about keeping their neighbourhoods clean than about social responsibility.

The importance of 'home' to the housed population seems obvious: consider the current abundance of interior and gardening stores and magazines, or the popularity of books such as Witold Rybczynski's *Home*. Many cultural theorists discuss the significance of home as the most immediate environment in which the construction of personal identity through control over one's own body takes place. In this context, homelessness can be defined as 'a dramatic loss of power over the way in which one's identity is constructed, since the home no longer shields from the public gaze.'[3]

At the same time, public housing projects themselves have notably failed to shield from the public gaze. 20th-century public housing endeavours to structure occupants' private lives in their entirety. Whoever has the power to structure the space in which people's lives take place also determines the ways in which the relations of production within a particular community can, or cannot, be contested; and the belief that spacious and hygienic living conditions should function to ensure contented, productive workers and citizens remains the unacknowledged motive of many housing activists today.[4] This priority keeps those who cannot work homeless, posing a muted challenge to a paternalistic model of society. Any serious attempt to reduce the number of homeless people then requires openness to different models of social organisation demanding new types of spatial organisation.

I have selected three types of project to accompany this text in order to shed light on various ways in which architects can be involved in schemes for the homeless. Both the Simone Hotel and the Boyd Hotel by Koning Eizenberg exemplify architects' typical responses and raise doubts as to their appropriateness. Working within the constraints of their briefs, Koning Eizenberg have proved that inventive design and affordable design are not mutually exclusive. Nevertheless, the buildings could not be less welcoming: no people, no personal belongings, in fact nothing at all would indicate habitation. The buildings do not seem to foster a sense of home, pride or community for inhabitants, nor do they encourage connections with those outside.

When I asked Julie Eizenberg how they dealt with the traditionally patronising attitude towards designing for the socially underprivileged, she answered that – faced with the problem of not knowing the individual needs of future residents – their approach was to think of homeless people as equal human beings and accordingly create an environment that they themselves would feel comfortable in. With the Skid Row Housing Trust managing the project and serving as an interface between the architects and the buildings' eventual occupants, Koning Eizenberg saw as their only option a strategy of de-institutionalisation through the manipulation of formal elements. Following the criticism of post-Second World War social housing, the failure of which has largely been blamed on architects taking on the role of social engineers, Koning Eizenberg's approach is symptomatic of many contemporary architects' fear of committing their work to a strong political or social agenda. However, both the Simone and the Boyd Hotel demonstrate that an architecture of aesthetic gestures cannot provide the environment for a solution to social problems.

While it is difficult to compare projects of such contrasting scales, SAMOSHELL, the structure designed by Zeballos + Smulevich, demonstrates that architectural services can be provided in a way that is very effective. Of course, their situation was different: first, the limitations of building a temporary structure in an extremely short amount of time for very little money provoked them into abandoning architects' desire to create original pieces and instead let them realise the opportunities of prefabricated structures in this context; and second, the architects were approached by a Santa Monica agency rather than the Salvation Army with the result that they became chief co-ordinators of the project serving as the interface between all parties involved. Zeballos + Smulevich also had access to likely future residents who at the time were already using SWASHLOCK, thus enabling the architects to develop a building that would take into consideration homeless people's needs as much as the requirements of the institution that would manage the shelter.

Yet despite its success, SAMOSHELL inspires general questions about the housed population's response to homelessness. Away from any residential neighbourhoods, the shelter is located on a property directly adjacent to the freeway. Entirely enclosed by a fence and camouflaged in Santa Monica's official blue-and-white colour scheme, it exists unnoticeably amongst the surrounding public structures. While this arrangement creates privacy for the homeless who choose to use the facility, it also effectively removes the unpleasant fact of homelessness from public view.

My final example is firmly rooted in Buckminster Fuller's motto: 'to make the world work in the shortest possible time through spontaneous co-operation without ecological offence or the disadvantage of anyone.' Genesis I Transitional Village's tradition is that of the mobile home park; while it did not and will not win any architectural awards it has nonetheless received more media attention than either of the other projects. The 'dome village' really raises two questions: whether professional architects can and should be involved in projects that necessitate a new attitude towards the production of space, and whether a temporary housing solution can actually subvert architects' conventional notions of living permanently.

The project's aim was not to provide shelter that was beautiful in any conventional sense, but to create a place that a group of homeless people would be able to call their own by making it so simple that it could be built by themselves. Three years later only a fraction of the original home builders are left, but current residents continue to improve on the village. They take pride in their achievement and like to show it off. Neighbours of Genesis I have expressed their appreciation of the project, and some researchers consider it a highly successful demonstration of how vital self-determination is to the homeless with respect to creating places that allow movement back into mainstream society.[5] Others describe the project as a failure. The village apparently has a low turnover rate; also, its independence inspires fear in some that it may provide a breeding ground for criminal activities.

Where earlier sociological texts are inclined to see the homeless as voluntary drop-outs from mainstream society,[6] later texts lean towards depicting them as helpless victims of fate.[7] As Rob Rosenthal argues, 'the emphasis changed from the "agency" of homeless people themselves – that is, their individual actions and behaviours – to the "constraints" imposed on them by social processes beyond their individual control.'[8] Yet both attitudes reflect the romantic belief that all homeless persons are socially isolated vagabonds or nomads.

This belief can lead to gross generalisations about the needs of the homeless. Rosenthal describes the homeless as a heterogeneous group that does not share many characteristics besides the one of having lost a permanent residence. He identifies six subgroups that each form their own social networks and often do not interact with each other. Architects have not been sensitive to this heterogeneity. For instance, none of the projects described cater to the need of a very large group of the homeless: families and single women with children. Few places target these groups

because they tend to lead a less visible, peripatetic existence, relying on the generosity of relatives and friends to share their homes.

Moreover, while many homeless people share mainstream aspirations, their requirements and expectations on the way to fulfilling those aspirations will differ significantly from those of the housed population. Architects' difficulty in accepting this difference is evident in the criticism of Genesis I. Despite the fact that mobile homes are the predominant form of unsubsidised affordable housing, they are still not widely appreciated because they do not fulfil the mainstream American demand for conventionally constructed dwellings.[9] Such standards of acceptability are preserved by private and public institutions such as mortgage bankers, zoning and building authorities, state and federal housing agencies and, of course, professional organisations of architects. These institutions are less interested in finding new models for living than in ensuring the predictability of the market through the protection of market values.[10] Housing reformers may create public support for responsible capitalism but, as I suggested earlier, they are simultaneously complicit with a system that has historically given housing not to the poorest but to workers. As a result they ensure that housing is produced by institutions that completely control the planning process in an attempt to create rationalised environments necessary for the preservation of the existing social order.

The difficulties to be overcome for architects in trying to find successful solutions for housing the homeless generate more general questions concerning the significance of architecture for housing. Rybczynski claims that the impact of architects is negligible in relation to the way most people live. By turning away from an involvement in mass production in the 1930s and concentrating on the image of the architect as artist, the architectural profession has deprived itself of the knowledge needed to produce good housing. The majority of people in the United States and Canada see no connection between architects and their private living environment. This should come as no surprise: 20th-century avant-garde architectural theory, which continues to dominate contemporary architectural teaching and discourse, is inherently anti-domestic. The ultimate validation for being modern is to despise the function of the home as a refuge and to deny its occupants' needs for privacy in which to develop and define individual and family identity.[11]

Significantly, none of the articles I found on either the Simone or the Boyd projects discuss the social connotations of Koning Eizenberg's designs. Instead, they assure us that our compassionate liberal souls may rest in peace now that the homeless can relax in surroundings straight out of a tasteful architectural or interior design magazine. SAMOSHELL and Genesis I, on the other hand, are projects that challenge accepted architectural paradigms. They are both projects that would not usually find their way onto the pages of a design-oriented architecture magazine because their original design is not what makes them interesting. In contrast to the interior of the Boyd Hotel – which still looks untouched a full year after opening – SAMOSHELL and Genesis I constitute an architecture of the everyday in which the process of appropriation by inhabitants and their daily needs overwhelms any concern with aesthetics. They provide shelter that allows identity to be established as a result of inhabitation

rather than design. The difference between the Simone and Boyd Hotels and projects such as SAMOSHELL and Genesis I is perhaps best expressed by saying that one approach exemplifies the desire of modern architects to stage the life of their clients, whereas the other approach is characterised by the flexibility necessary to enable inhabitants to define and live their particular differences.

Notes

1 It requires each state to have 30 per cent of welfare recipients either engaged in work or enrolled in work training by the end of 1998. While this goal may be reached in rural and suburban areas it appears elusive in cities where the welfare population is concentrated.

2 Jennifer Wolch, 'From Global to Local: The Rise of Homelessness in Los Angeles during the 1980s', Allen J Scott and Edward W Soja (eds), *The City: Los Angeles and Urban Theory at the End of the Twentieth Century*, University of California Press (Berkeley, Los Angeles and London), 1996, pp390-425.

3 Neil Smith, 'Homeless/Global: Scaling places', Jon Bird et al (eds), *Mapping the Futures: Local Cultures, Global Change*, Routledge (London and New York), 1993, pp87-119.

4 Don Mitchell, 'Public Housing in Single-Industry Towns: Changing Landscapes of Paternalism', in James Duncan and David Ley, *Place/Culture/Representation*, Routledge (London and New York), 1994, pp110-27.

5 See, for instance, Michael Dear and Jurgen von Mahs, 'Housing for the Homeless, by the Homeless, and of the Homeless', in Nan Ellin (ed), *Architecture of Fear*, Princeton Architectural Press (New York), 1997, pp187-200.

6 See, for example, Jacob A Riis, *How the Other Half Lives*, Hill and Wang (New York), 1957, orig pub 1890, p148: 'It is a mistake to think that they are helpless little creatures, to be pitied and cried over because they are alone in the world. [. . .] The *Street Arab* has all the faults and all the virtues of the lawless life he leads. *Vagabond* that he is, acknowledging no authority and owning no allegiance to anybody or anything, with his grimy fist raised against society whenever it tries to coerce him, he is as bright and sharp as a weasel, which among all the predatory beasts, he most resembles' (my emphasis).

7 See, for example, Alexander Cockburn, 'On the Rim of the Pacific Century', in David Reid (ed), *Sex, Death and God in L.A.*, University of California Press

(Berkeley and Los Angeles), 1992, p10: 'In the interval of a couple of blocks we could see the class war fought out at the level of the built environment. Amid the corporate towers of the prime redevelopment zones there were pleasant little spaces, gardens, bowers amid the reflecting glass, along with avant-garde street furniture inviting you to linger and repose. Move toward skid row, and the destitute *urban nomad* pushing his purloined shopping cart finds himself the object of low-intensity civic warfare: rounded bus seats he can't lie down on, sprinkler system drenching areas where he might sleep, spikes and bars guarding trash he might try to sort through' (my emphasis).

8 Rob Rosenthal, *Homeless in Paradise: A Map of the Terrain*, Temple University Press (Philadelphia), 1994, p3.

9 Allan D Wallis, *Wheel Estate: The Rise and Decline of Mobile Homes*, The Johns Hopkins University Press (Baltimore & London), 1991, pp12-29.

10 To give just two examples of many I mention the following:
In a recent exhibition about new models of housing in Los Angeles, Re: American Dream, architects demonstrate how to maximise the use of down-sized city lots while the underlying ideology of ownership, privacy and individuality remains untouched;
The Department of Housing and Urban Development's new policy is not to built emergency shelters nor to improve existing bad housing but to reconstruct entire neighbourhoods based on New Urbanist principles that consist of rules such as: mixed-use developments, access to public transport, pedestrian friendly streets and last but not least the construction of traditional brick town houses with columns, gabled roofs, etc.

11 Christopher Reed, 'Introduction', in Christopher Reed (ed), *Not at Home: The Suppression of Domesticity in Modern Art and Architecture*, Thames and Hudson (London), 1996, pp7-17.

Zeballos + Smulevich, SAMOSHELL, Santa Monica Homeless Shelter, Los Angeles, 1994

SAMOSHELL

In 1994 a law was passed that prohibited sleeping in public spaces; an emergency shelter to house those affected by the new law was needed urgently. Santa Monica's Human Affairs Division contacted architects Zeballos + Smulevich who in 1993 had re-designed a group of existing buildings to serve as a shower/laundry/locker-storage facility, SWASHLOCK, for the City of Santa Monica SAMOSHELL, the Santa Monica Homeless Shelter, would be built on the same property – leased for a temporary period from the Santa Monica Department of Transportation. Several Santa Monica agencies participated in the design and construction, collaborating with Sprung Instant Structures Inc. of Calgary, Canada, the architects, and the Salvation Army, who would ultimately manage the shelter.

The project had to be completed within a four-month period, so a pre-engineered structure seemed the only feasible solution. Sprung Instant Structures' system consists of aluminium wide flange members spaced ten-feet apart and bolted on to a concrete slab. Once the vinyl stressed skin membrane is stretched over this skeleton, it forms a 37x18 metre lightweight shell. Attempting to domesticise the scale of the building,

the architects modified the manufacturer's standard CAD shop drawings to include translucent panels at window height as well as a series of 'dormer windows' at a higher level. Inside the vaulted structure, human scale is achieved through the height of partitions, suspended ventilation and fluorescent lighting.

Space for communal activities is located between the building's entrance and an office area in the back. Altogether the structure provides shelter for 100 people of both sexes. The intention was to separate women's and men's sleeping quarters by a box-shaped volume containing restroom and washing facilities. Yet due to an increase in the number of homeless women seeking shelter, the general sleeping area has now been partitioned into two spaces. Besides designing the shelter and managing its construction, Zeballos + Smulevich obtained used commercial kitchen equipment, second-hand storage lockers, and beds from military surplus.

Genesis I Transitional Village

This is located a few blocks west of Los Angeles' downtown financial district. A corporate grant, the help of downtown property developer David Adams and the

approval of both mayor's office and city council enabled homeless activist Ted Hayes, founder of Justiceville/Homeless USA, to begin constructing 18 domes that would house the experimental community he had envisaged. The structures are engineer Craig Chamberlain's variation on Buckminster Fuller's geodesic dome. They are bolted together from curved non-toxic polyester fibreglass panels that sit on a concrete footing. They take about two hours to built, are earthquake and water proof and, at the time, cost approximately $6,500 each.

Twelve domes house two residents each. The other domes accommodate communal kitchen, office, storage and meeting space. Governed by the conviction that the 'best form of government is self government', residents must show both willingness to stabilise their lives and commitment to supporting the village. Responsibility for management, maintenance of personal and property appearance and village security are supposed to improve organisational abilities and imbue homeless people with a sense of self-esteem and self-reliance. The village is also linked with social agencies that provide counselling and work-related services.

Genesis I Transitional Village, Los Angeles, 1993

REWI THOMPSON
FOUR PROJECTS

Rewi Thompson's architecture takes a challenging and at the same time accessible approach to dealing with issues of the everyday. Rewi's work commits itself to taking a social and political stance within New Zealand's unique cultural framework. The issue of biculturalism is particularly relevant to contemporary New Zealand. Bicultural architecture does not have a strong history and Rewi's projects attempt to broach this topic introducing its presence both physically and metaphysically. The treaty of Waitangi, an agreement dealing with equal rights, land ownership and sovereignty, drawn up between the Maori chiefs and the Crown in 1840, has only recently begun to be acknowledged by New Zealand's government. The strong and conflicting opinions of the colonialists or Pakeha (the visitors) and the Tangata Whenua (people of the land) are evident in their approach to dealing with everyday issues. Rewi's work attempts to unite the two cultural frameworks, acknowledging their differences and making use of the dynamic which their juxtaposition creates. This approach brings a raw and youthful feeling to his work. Such an energy is commonly felt by New Zealanders as the realisation of the need to acknowledge the past and deal

with its effects on the future becomes stronger, but it is seldom dealt with architecturally.

Rewi's work appears to challenge conventional architectural practice in the way that it tackles big issues without finding the need to create a monumental architecture to complement them. Just as Rewi's approach is holistic, considering site, materials, form and brief from a physical and metaphysical viewpoint, his buildings are inherently powerful because there is a consideration of every part and its philosophical as well as visual or tactile accompaniment. Attention to the assembly of everyday aspects of architecture creates the enigma, rather than a more traditional approach where attention to outstanding elements creates power through the extraordinary.

Throughout the following projects examples will be shown of how cultural frameworks, protocol and rituals are woven into the physical and conceptual aspects of Rewi's projects, and how consideration of social and cultural aspects of contemporary New Zealand has become a 'natural part' of his dealings with the everyday.

Thompson Residence

The Thompson house recognises differing attitudes in relation to Auckland's past and anticipates the possible effects that these will have on social and political directions in the future. The unfinished and exposed quality of its materials acknowledge the benefits of change and reconciliation; while the staunch formal presence makes it clear that the right to freedom of personal expression will not be negotiated into mediocrity.

Although existing as a residential-scale personal statement, the house has represented a challenge to its conservative neighbourhood. The materials used – plywood and concrete block – recall something from outside the realm of consciousness of the Thompson's neighbours; something which is seen as a protest or resistance. The house was never intended to appear aggressive towards its neighbours. The purpose of the confrontational facade is a comment by the Thompsons on how houses in Auckland engage, or avoid engaging, with their community and broader site. The delicate patterning of the plain faced ply, makes no attempt to hide the wrinkles and cracks in its skin – hinting at an undercurrent of irritation and anticipation

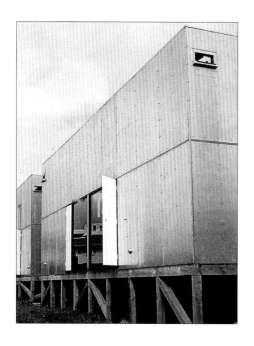

OPPOSITE: Thompson House, Kohimarama, Auckland, New Zealand; THIS PAGE: Puukenga, Maori Education Centre, Auckland, New Zealand

of the inhabitants. For the family the house intensifies the dynamics of everyday concepts of *whanau*.[1] The singular form encompassing the interior spaces as a whole, rather than a series, restores unity to the family and offers it a protected space within which its expectations and dreams can be cultivated. In this way the house acts as a vehicle for the aspirations of the *whanau*.

Puukenga, Maori Education Centre at Carrington Polytechnic

Puukenga's presence initiates a challenge to the existing bureaucracy surrounding the 'conventional' design process of educational institutions. The competition brief for Puukenga called for an architect who understood Maori protocol and rituals, and also the need to work closely with the *Kaumatua*,[2] the Elders, staff, and others involved with the development of the institution. The strong communication between the broad client base, who knew what they wanted, and the architect, filling the role of facilitator, had a definite impact on the focus of the project. Ultimately this communication translated into a coherent and functional design which responded both to the physical and philosophical demands of

the brief. Far from limiting the architect's creative licence, his role assumed a much broader perspective, which inspired and educated his decisions throughout the design

The concept of Puukenga encompasses focus and growth. Alongside the need to fulfil educational requirements, the building had to possess a dynamic between itself and its community so pathways would be created for the spread and reception of knowledge. For example welcoming people needed to be formalised as an inherent ritual within the structure.

The traditional role of women on the *Marae*[3] of welcoming visitors with a *Karanga*,[4] is demonstrated formally and through the tactility of materials chosen. Wooden boards take on a sculptural effect which emphasises the passage and the curved walls of the entrance, as well as possessing a metaphorical link to weaving and *Tuku Tuku* panels.[5] Focus and extension between the physical and metaphysical worlds are expressed by the conduit which links the architectural space internally with the exterior.

Having passed through the embrace of the woman the central focus of the building is the *Pouihi*.[6] The carved

ancestral figures of the *Pouihi* relate to genealogies and histories concerning the retrieval of the three baskets of knowledge, the separation of Papatuanuku (the Earth Mother) and Ranginui (the Sky Father), to let light into the world, and more. The *Pouihi* also marks the interstitial space between the instinctively warm entrance of the woman and the rational, almost industrially conceived teaching spaces denoting the male attributes. These boxes of rational thought, clad in galvanised steel panels and supported off the ground by exposed tanalised timber foundations are placed protectively around the sacred *Pouihi* and the supple female domain. The juxtaposition of form and materials relates to the equal importance of the male and female roles.

In place of a written history, the tradition of the Maori is to embed their stories and genealogies into the fabric and structure of their buildings. The architecture itself retains the knowledge through *Tuku Tuku*, and wall and post carvings. This idea is translated into the architecture of Puukenga. Even if you are unfamiliar with Maori tradition, the realisation of underlying philosophical concepts into strong formal and materialistic systems has resulted in a stylistic challenge for the commonplace educational institution.

The building receives the utmost respect from its users. Students and staff who have participated in the whole process of Puukenga from conception, through to completion and on-going functioning, remove their shoes before entering the school. Just as the foundations create a new ground to build on, Puukenga carries within it the beginnings of a different focus, fitted within a traditional institutional framework. As part of a system, hopefully its influence will spread. Puukenga delivers a humble but forceful example to the short history of bicultural architecture.

Rata Vine Housing Project
Within their tradition of state-funded housing, the contemporary sites of Manukau and Auckland possess a sprawl of individual houses with little respect paid to collective identity or coherent planning strategy. Creation of sustainable communities should be one of the dominating issues of these housing projects.

The approach to this project was the same as it would have been for any other client. Rather than concentrating on the economic status of the prospective residents, focus was centred on design

and facilitating basic needs, in a physical as well as a philosophical or social sense.

With Rata Vine, Rewi tried to create a development aware of communal and public spaces and able to create a strong visual impact of unity, whilst still maintaining aesthetic differences between the individual houses. To achieve this aim Rewi's holistic approach applied the above ideas to structural form, landscaping, materials and services. Keeping vehicular access and parking central allowed for exploration of formal and landscaping possibilities. The result achieved privacy between the dwellings while still maintaining an overall aesthetic, readily relating back to the natural contours and previous identity of the site, which used to be farm land.

Also reminiscent of the site's history are the materials. Galvanised steel and wire are part of New Zealand culture. As a farming nation they are familiar materials in areas where the landscape is divided and wrapped by barbed wire and electricity pylons. An everyday material able to withstand the environmental forces, raw galvanised steel may be crude, but it is not attempting to cover up its actions. Its presence is strong and its function easily understood.

Once New Zealand possessed the promise of unlimited possibilities, both for the Maori and the Pakeha. Today, as the wild landscape becomes increasingly stratified, issues of land and ownership are a dominant topic in political discussions. These divisions of the land need to be acknowledged, before they translate, any further, into divisions between people.

Wishart House
Ever since the first colonials arrived in New Zealand there have been reports of its amazing picturesque landscape. Some pioneers arrived only to feel betrayed; the image of paradise having been shattered by the savage intensity of its natural forces. For others, the reality offered more than the original image could ever have dreamed of imparting. It is no wonder New Zealanders feel such an affinity to their land – the power of its presence is indescribable.

Ironically the idea of architecture trying to engage with the landscape, as an initial concept for a house, is often considered by the architectural institutions as a cliché, and insufficient grounds for design. Unfortunately, this limits many design considerations concerning the landscape to issues of view.

The Wishart house creates a dialogue

with the awesome energy of the site, an exposed section at the mercy of the coastal elements. Rather than creating a solid house which stoically keeps its space to itself in an attempt at protection from the harsh elements, architect and client decided to take up the challenge, thrusting their built environment into the reception of these forces.

The idea was to create a simple space of floor, roof and walls; then to create a structure around it. (As opposed to dealing with the forces in terms of the structure and then filling it with elements.) The selected space is surrounded by views of a harbour opening out to the Tasman Sea, sand dunes and native bush; all made dynamic by the frequently changing weather conditions playing with colour and texture.

An elevated deck/stage was created with walls that also lift off the ground, helping to shield and contain views. The walls serve psychological as well as physical purposes. Through their placement certain aspects of the differing views are ignored forcing you to acknowledge and/or contemplate their absence. In this way rather than engulfing a person with the spectacular, the withheld view acts as a stabilising influence on their thinking about nature and our treatment

of it. They are forced to move themselves if they want to see it all.

Actual contact with nature is expressed quite dramatically. Although spatially direct, the structural elements defining the space fight to achieve this directness. Walls and roof distort and kink as evidence to the dramatic tension which their bracing fixtures must endure.

The interior divisions are defined by the crossing paths of views which enter through the splaying out of the wall planes at either end of the main form. These lines of intersection will also nominate the placement of storage and services. Lighting will also be accommodated for separately. In this way the unavoidable chaos of 'regular' lighting fixtures will not need to enter the domestic scene. The inhabitants can create the lighting as they please; and the walls are left unscathed.

Some of these partitioning boxes will be partly made from glass, half-filled with sand from the dunes; the remaining space could be occupied by the finds collected on bush walks. This containment of nature is a reminder of its continual presence and the impact of its energy and forces – not only on the people but also on the built form and materials.

Notes
1 *Whanau* represents a singular space for unity and family.
2 Respected male elder/teacher.
3 Community meeting place of Maori tradition.
4 Call on to the *Marae* sung by women.
5 *Tuku Tuku* are woven wall panels in traditional Maori buildings, the strong geometrical patterns of which are of specific meaning.
6 A *Pouihi* is similar to a totem pole. Here the carved ancestral figures represent different principles of humanity.

OPPOSITE: Rata Vine Housing Project; BELOW L to R: Wishart House, Hokianga, under construction; model

1

2   *Sinte Gleska University, FROM ABOVE: Landscape; Hexagon Building*

CLARK STEVENS

EVERYDAY OBSERVATIONS

Sinte Gleska University and RoTo Architects

RoTo was founded in 1991 to navigate, explore and exploit the uncertainty of the conditions of the 'everyday' in the pursuit of architectural ideas. Our working process develops a particular language of form and human relations for each project based upon aggressive and continuous research of the natural and social conditions that form the spatial condition of the everyday.

A collaborative approach to the authorship of our work is guided by a respect for and celebration of individual knowledge, talent and experience. We have assembled an organisation of individuals who share a generosity of spirit and yet maintain divergent formal skills and world views. The openness within RoTo has also made it possible for us to collaborate in a genuine sense with those who commission and inhabit the architecture we facilitate. We enthusiastically embrace found conditions and conventions as an opportunity for improvisation.

Since the spring of 1994, we have been funded by the Lannan Foundation Indigenous Communities Program to plan and build a new campus for Sinte Gleska University. Sinte is the oldest tribal university in the Americas, founded 25 years ago by the Sicangu Lakota in Rosebud, South Dakota. When we first came to the Rosebud Reservation to begin our campus planning work, we felt that we were unable to ask the right questions, and the Lakota people seemed to be unable to tell us what they wanted. Perhaps they were unable to tell us because nobody had asked them before, but it is more likely that they knew exactly what they valued and chose not to say. I suspect that they felt that we, in light of their cultural and life experiences, were not to be trusted with that knowledge.

Planning, programming and community design techniques for architects have traditionally centred around collective exercises, structured to quickly obtain facts and data from representative client and 'user' groups. They typically rely on the tendency of individuals (generally white male individuals) to state their personal opinions freely. Certain architectural firms have developed elaborate 'facilitation' methods to encourage, coerce or otherwise extract enough information to start drawing in as short a timeframe as possible. I recall from my professional practice courses that one well-known firm called such exercises 'squatter sessions', a wildly inappropriate term in the context of a people who lost their way of life to a squatter culture.

After a few relatively unsuccessful attempts at conventional programming, we ultimately did what we do in our office when thought alone fails to produce an answer: we made something. Not a building of our own design, but something that an individual member of the Lakota community had needed, planned and brought into being by sheer energy and force of will. Two of us went and lived and worked for a week and built, along with a dozen Native American men, women, and children, a 16 x 24 foot straw-bale house for a tribal elder. While we were there, we heard stories, jokes and myths. We learned a bit about how we should act and what was expected of us.

After we helped to build Grandma Little Elk's house, we were told of modular building components available from defence contractors that were being downsized. Experimenting with four 12 x 60 inch modules, we adapted the straw-bale techniques we had learned to complete an existing campus building that had lost its funding in the late 1970s. In the process we helped to reactivate the Tribal sawmill and provided an opportunity for the community to gain construction experience. Our construction crew was the maintenance department of Sinte Gleska University and the ninth grade boys' basketball team of the St Francis Indian School.

We spent many hours in the next year with the people of the Sicangu Lakota Nation getting to know them and absorbing their landscape. We continued to build as we learned, and we began to know what to look for because we *engaged* with the place. We participated in systems, natural and cultural, that were not of our making or under our control before we proposed any permanent alterations to the landscape at the new campus. Our understanding derived from engaged listening and active participation. We did not import an aesthetic system that was derived from elsewhere. (**2,4-7**)

By coincidence, my own family has had a tradition of spending a week in South Dakota every year since I was a boy. I first came to this land when I was ten years old and have returned every year since with my brothers and

3

4

FROM ABOVE: Grandma Elk's House; Hexagon Building, Sinte Gleska University

5

6

7

Hexagon Building, Sinte Gleska University

my father. Before I understood that there were Native Americans and Americans, I began to understand the land.

Over the years, as I visited each fall, my perception of the place changed. A landscape that had at first seemed flat and empty transformed into a place that contained an immense variety of life and spaces. I noticed that living things, whether they crawled or flew, walked on two legs or four, were most comfortable in very particular types of prairie spaces. These spaces were forms initially indistinguishable from the spaces adjacent to them. After years of such observations, it now seems to me that life is not 'found' in these spaces, it is made from and of them: the pheasant is made from the space that divides the dense yellow shortgrass prairie from the more open stand of blood red rosehips. The pheasant is the boundary and the blending of the earth, sky, prairie grass and rosehips. The grouse grows from the chokecherry tree and the chokecherry tree is made of the concave space where the base of a bluff becomes the base of the next. What I have learned about Lakota cosmology has reinforced this understanding of space. (**1,8,11,12**)

My goal in all of our work is to produce an indigenous architecture of the present day that is as inevitable a completion of its context as the trout is of the eddy behind the rock. I am beginning to think that becoming 'native' or indigenous has as much or more to do with learning to be conscious and respectful of the natural world than it does with blood ancestry or cultural inheritance. It also involves learning that human systems are only a subset of natural systems, and that our technologies, including building technologies, should be applied with a sense of balance and restraint.

We have found that gradual transformation of the known and familiar made the built results of the process more meaningful and valued in the community. Being respectful of the 'comfort level' of the people and place in which we worked not only allowed all the collaborators in the process to develop a proprietary interest in the results, but also kept us from missing the opportunities of generic conditions. Even the most mundane and conventional aspects of the everyday provided opportunities to access larger systems of meaning.

Our approach to learning in a context dominated by landscape and cultural history has been to look for the values and abstract systems of order inherent in the reality of the place. Not to act as 'preservationists' of some Disney ideal, but to look at the contemporary condition and find links to traditional, organic and integrated systems of values. We look for tangencies that connect the social to the technological to the natural, within the framework of reciprocity that is the basis of an indigenous understanding of the universe. Many of the people of the Rosebud remain there because they know that human beings complete the natural world by engaging that world responsibly. They have reinforced my belief that by knowing a place through engagement, participation and listening to the conditions of the everyday, the things that we build can complete the intentions of a place. (**9,10**)

Our techniques for identifying the programme, location and form of contemporary indigenous architecture at Sinte Gleska began with a mapping of the relationships that were described to us: earth to sky, people to earth, sons-in-law to mothers-in-law, river to willows. We mapped the

8

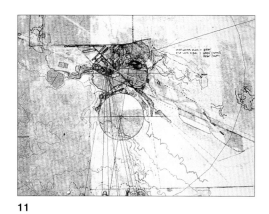

11

9

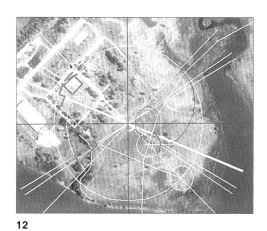

12

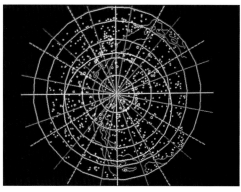

13

*Sinte Gleska University, LEFT FROM
ABOVE: Landscape; Technology
Building; RIGHT FROM ABOVE:
Campus plans; siting study*

10

69

14

17

15

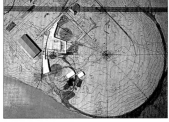

16

Sinte Gleska University, FROM ABOVE: Technology Building; campus plans

relationships that connected story to place. (**13**)

When we presented these maps to the Lakota people – our attempt at campus planning – we were afraid that they would be perceived as mundane, presumptuous, arrogant or irrelevant. They were, in fact, received as if they were a part of history that the people and the community had always known. They were pleased that we were finally catching on. (**14**)

Learning was reciprocal. At first they said, 'build us circles, not squares'. As we became more comfortable with one another, we reminded them that the land contained many forms, and that the stories they had told us contained spaces that were deserving of more study. Their knowledge demanded a more considered approach to a permanent alteration of their landscape than picturesque reproductions of traditional shelters could accomplish. Nevertheless, we began to see circles in the land. (**15,16**)

We grappled sincerely with the notion of 'community design', because of the history of outsider impact on Lakota culture. Eventually we found a balance between our desire to act as architects, and our commitment to give the people a voice. We also found a Lakota cultural precedent that helped us to better define our role. In the Lakota *tiospaye*, or extended family, an individual's position (which is not quite an appropriate term) is determined not by skills, gifts, talents or knowledge, but rather by the generosity with those particular abilities that are shared for the good of the community, or *tiospaye*, and not just for the existing community; the

Lakota always speak of the impact that their decisions and actions have on the next seven generations. (**17,19**)

Suppression of one's individuality is not required to be a good *tiospaye* member. Not every individual has been given the vision of a warrior, a healer or an architect. The only imperative is that an individual does not use his gifts to satisfy his individual desires at the expense of the *tiospaye*. Lakota values do not confuse individualism with selfishness like the culture that replaced them in North America. Traditional Lakota had an expectation that those who were gifted would act in the best interests of all, which gave them the power of faith.

In the 1990s, however, there no longer exists the integration of nature, art, culture, war and love that produced and was produced by those traditional values. Our shared process aspires to those values, even as it deals with the pettiness of small-town relations, bad weather, lack of skills, shortage of hope, the limitations and opportunities of local conventions, crumbling infrastructure, and 80-per-cent unemployment. (**18**)

We once asked Paul Leader-Charge, a 99-year-old Lakota elder, how the Lakota people had known to locate and move their camps. We expected that his answer would reveal one of the clues to the Lakota version of 'feng shui'. Instead, he answered in the terms of the everyday: 'We are clean people. When the latrines were full, it was time to go'.

Numbers in brackets refer to images.

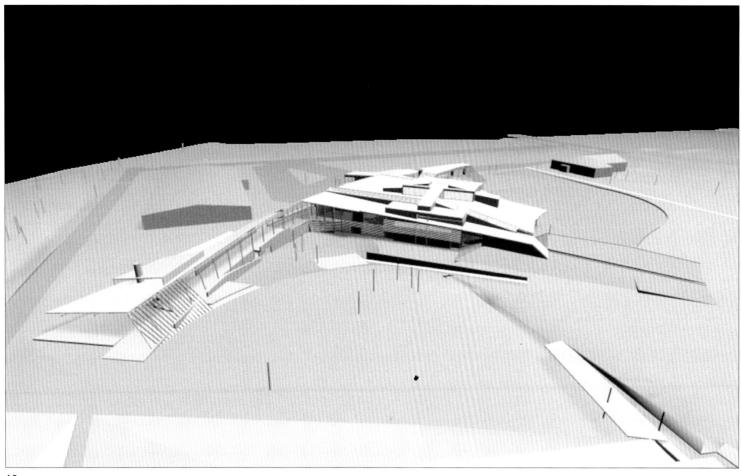

18

19 *Sinte Gleska University, FROM ABOVE: Multipurpose Building; Technology Building*

SAMUEL MOCKBEE
THE RURAL STUDIO

For every architect there is a creative moment when he or she plugs into the Muse and generates, from Chaos, a sketch that builds order. The sketch is a mark that suggests the possibility of an idea and an ideal. Taking this act further and applying it to all of us is about making some mark in one's lifetime that can be given the title of Architecture; a mark that will remain after the power of one's living imagination is gone.

All architects expect and hope their work will act in some sense as a servant for humanity – to make a better world. That is the search we should always be undertaking and, again, there are no clear-cut definitions or assumed pathways. Therefore it is important to give critical attention to some basic issues that every architect, regardless of time and place, will have to face. Issues that Alberti called choosing between fortune and virtue. Issues not as questions of judgment but questions of value and principle. What I am going to try and show is my own search in dealing with these issues.

Architects are by nature and pursuit leaders and teachers. If architecture is going to inspire a community, or stimulate the status quo into making responsible environmental and social structural changes now and in the future, it will take what I call the 'subversive leadership' of academicians and practitioners to remind the student of architecture that theory and practice are not only interwoven with one's culture but with the responsibility of shaping the environment, of breaking up social complacency, and challenging the power of the status quo.

Last year, I was asked to participate in an AIA (American Institute of Architects) Design Conference, along with two other architects and the English architect Michael Hopkins. Each of us gave lectures during the day and then participated in an after-dinner panel discussion that evening. Primarily, the questions-and-answers session that evening settled around questions about how an architect receives and executes major commissions. Each of the other architects were giving their answers to this question when Michael Hopkins interjected somewhat matter-of-factly that the evening before he had received a 'fax on his pillow' informing him that he had just received yet another commission from one of his major clients in England.

Later on someone made the observation that Hopkins was working for the richest woman in the world – the Queen of England – while I was working for the poorest man in the world, Shepard Bryant (the client and recipient of The Rural Studio's first charity house, the Hay Bale House in Mason's Bend, Alabama). They noted at the same time that my work and the work of Michael Hopkins represented two very different approaches to the practice of architecture. They wondered what the implications of this were. The question was directed at me and I answered that it probably had more to do with our nature than with any convictions – more to do with our own private (and somewhat selfish) desires rather than any commitment to public virtue. But as far as my own convictions went, I believe that architects are given a gift of second sight and when we see something that others can't we should act, and we shouldn't wait for decisions to be made by politicians or multinational corporations. Architects should always be in the initial critical decision-making position in order to challenge the power of the status quo. We need to understand that when a decision is made, a position has already been taken. Architects should not be consigned to only problem-solving after the fact.

People then turned to Michael Hopkins for his answer. He replied, 'Maybe architects shouldn't be in the position to make those kinds of decisions.' I took this to mean issues affecting social, economic, political or environmental decisions, and also staying away from making subversive decisions!

At first I was somewhat stunned by his answer and then reflected that perhaps here was a man who could be speaking for most practising architects.

I do not believe that courage has gone out of the profession, but we tend to be narrow in the scope of our thinking and underestimate our natural capacity to be subversive leaders and teachers. In other words, the more we practise, the more restricted we become in our critical thinking and our life styles. Critical thought requires looking beyond architecture towards an enhanced understanding of the whole to which it belongs. Accordingly, the role of architecture should be placed in relation to other issues of education, healthcare, transportation,

OPPOSITE: The Harris House, 1996-97, Greensboro, Alabama; grave of James Chaney, civil-rights worker

recreation, law enforcement, employment, the environment, the collective community that impacts on the lives of both the rich and the poor.

The political and environmental needs of our day require taking subversive leadership as well as an awareness that where you are, how you got there, and why you are still there, are more important than you think they are.

Architecture, more than any other art form, is a social art and must rest on the social and cultural base of its time and place. For those of us who design and build, we must do so with an awareness of a more socially responsive architecture. The practice of architecture not only requires participation in the profession but it also requires civic engagement. As a social art, architecture must be made where it is and out of what exists there. The dilemma for every architect is how to advance our profession and our

community with our talents rather than our talents being used to compromise them.

We must use the opportunity to survey our own backyards either to see what makes them special, individual and beautiful, or to note the unjust power of the status quo, or the indifference of the religious or intellectual community in dealing with social complacency or the nurturing of the environment. Peering out at your contemporary landscape is required before commitments to inspire can be started, accomplished and finished.

People and place matter. Architecture is a continually developing profession now under the influence of consumer-driven culture. The profession is becoming part of the corporate world and corporations (citizens of no place or any place) increasingly resemble nation states. Of the world's largest 100 economies, 49 are

countries and 51 are corporations. The 200 largest corporations employ only three-quarters of one percent of the world's work force.

During the next 25 years forces in the world of politics, economics and the environment will be driven by two factors: a demographic explosion that will double the population in undeveloped countries; and a technological explosion of robotics, biotechnology, lasers, optics and telecommunication in developed countries. These two factors will have a major impact on the natural environment. The architect's role will be to make architecture labour under the given conditions of a particular place, whether it is Winston County, Mississippi, Mason Bend, Alabama, or Mascot, Australia. It is not prudent to sit back as architects and rely on the corporate world's scientists and technology experts to decide which problems to solve. It is in the

architect's own interest to assert his or her values – values that respect, we should hope, the greater good.

It is also obvious that the place one is inspired by is of profound importance. The chance of not being from that place is not a crippling deficiency that will render one incapable of inspiration. What is important is using one's talent, intellect and energy in order to gain an appreciation and affection for people and place.

Architecture will make itself understood. There is something divine in a work of architecture, and we must maintain faith in the wonder of architecture to bring us into accord with the natural world, the supernatural world, with our fellow human beings and the great unknown.

I'd like to explain a little about my background – about being blessed and cursed as a

The Bryant House, 1995, Greensboro, Alabama; OVERLEAF: interior of the Bryant House

Southerner. Coleman Coker, my partner, and I grew up in North Mississippi. We are first cousins, six generations removed. As Southerners our heritage is part of our character. My great grandfather rode with the Mississippi Partisan Rangers under Colonel WC Falkner and later General Forrest. These were my heroes growing up in the segregated South of the 1950s and the early 1960s. I grew up recreating the great battles of Brices Crossroads and visiting the battlefields of Vicksburg and Shiloh.

Later I came to realise the contradictions that existed in my world. That I came from an isolated area where lies were being confronted with the truth. That I came from the American South which was attached to fiction and false values and a willingness to justify cruelty and injustice in the name of those values.

Years ago, I was outside my home at Meridan, Mississippi, and I had to pull over and stop for a road grader. While I was waiting I noticed a graveyard and a particular grave. It was the grave of James Chaney. James Chaney was one of three civil-rights workers killed in the summer of 1964. He would be a man of about my age today, but, more importantly, I have now come to believe and know that he defines who I am and who I am not. For me, he represents one of the true heroes of the South. And he is a true hero by the fact that he had the courage to risk his life and accept responsibility. His courage was a gift to me and to all of us. As architects we are given a gift and with it, a responsibility, though certainly more passive than James Chaney's. But the question for us is the same: do we have the courage to make our gift count for something?

The professional challenge, whether one is an architect in the rural American South or elsewhere in the world, is how to avoid being so stunned by the power of modern technology and economic affluence that one does not lose sight of the fact that people and place matter.

For me, drawing and painting are the initial influences for the making of architecture. The sketch is always out front. It sees ahead and deeper into what is already on the paper.

The initial sketch is always an emotion, not a concept. In the beginning, it is important to allow the imagination to move freely without any influence from a preconceived form. It's a mark that suggests the possibility of an idea. For me, it's the act of drawing that allows the hand to come into accord with the heart. When that happens, there comes a moment when the marks of the sketch – it can be a pen mark or a computer mark – utter the first deeper knowledge of what will come later.

This brings us to the present phase in my quest as an architect. Even though my career had been developing successfully, I did not feel

that I was maturing as a responsible architectural citizen. I believe what the poet William Carlos Williams prescribed about the best architect being the person 'with the most profound insight into the lives of the community'. So I applied to, and received, a Graham Foundation Grant to execute a series of large murals in an attempt to extend the study of architecture into what I hoped would be a wider human landscape. I am interested in what might prompt and make possible a process of entering a taboo landscape, in my case, the economic poverty of the Deep South; also in developing a discourse beyond merely looking at the effects of poverty but also at how architects can step over the threshold of injustice and address the true needs of a neglected American family and particularly the needs of their children. Of all Southerners, young children are the most likely to be living in poverty. In Mississippi, one in four lives below the poverty level. These children don't have the same advantages as the rest of America's children. They will come of age without any vision of how to rescue themselves from the curse of poverty.

Physical poverty is not an abstraction, but we almost never think of impoverishment as evidence of a world that exists. Much less do we imagine that it's a condition from which we may draw enlightenment in a very practical way. The paintings which began the work of the Rural Studio try to establish a discourse between those of us who have become mentally and morally stalled in modern obligations and these families who have no prospect of such obligations. The paintings are by no means an attempt to aestheticise poverty. It's about stepping across a social impasse into an honesty that refuses to gloss over inescapable facts. It's an honesty that permits differences to exist side by side with great tolerance and respect. Just as those of us who have had advantages can learn from this resilience, so can architecture learn something from an architecture of honesty. It is about stepping into the open and expressing the simple and the actual rather than the grand and the ostentatious. It's not about your greatness as an architect but about your compassion.

These paintings are an attempt at becoming an agency of understanding what is common and universal for all families. Architecture won't begin to alleviate all of these social woes. But what is necessary is a willingness to seek solutions to poverty in its own context, not outside it. What is required is the replacement of abstract opinions with knowledge based on real human contact and personal realisation applied to the work and place.

This brings me to Auburn University's Rural Studio. It had become clear to me that if architectural education was going to play any socially-engaged role, it would be necessary to work with the segment of the profession that would one day be in a position to make decisions: the student. The main purpose of the Rural Studio is to enable each student to step across the threshold of misconceived opinions and to design/build with a 'moral sense' of service to a community. It is my hope that this experience will help the student of architecture to be more sensitive to the power and promise of what they do, to be more concerned with the good effects of architecture than with 'good intentions'. The Rural Studio represents an opportunity to be real in itself. The students become architects of their own education.

For me, these small projects have in them the architectural essence to enchant us, to inspire us, and ultimately, to elevate our profession. But more importantly, they remind us of what it means to have an American architecture without pretence. They remind us that we can be as awed by the simple as by the complex and that if we pay attention, this will offer us a glimpse into what is essential to the future of American Architecture: its honesty.

'Love your neighbour as yourself.' This is the most important thing because nothing else matters. In doing so, an architect will act on a foundation of decency which can be built upon. Go above and beyond the call of a 'smoothly functioning conscience'; help those who aren't likely to help you in return, and do so even if nobody is watching!

Paintings from the Rural Studio

A Shed, Zones B, Europan 4, 1996

LE K ARCHITECTURES
ALIVE, JUST THAT

The love of cities weaves itself in simple letters, in words gleaned from the chance encounter, in 'dreams of stones under the sun',[1] in the firmament of great cities and centuries. But the city dies. Between an urbanity saturated by rule-bound logic and a town highlighted by a myriad of reflections of a vanished past, the question of what constitutes urbanity remains.[2] But it is not so much the city that has changed nature, rather that man has changed the nature of the city.

The principal truth of architecture lies in its capacity to adopt the recesses, folds and modesties of a city, to seem absent in order to be more desired, to believe that 'life will always win'.

The city consists of fragments of intimacy, spaces secluded from ordinary usages, magical entanglements of love, hopes and broken destinies. The city is not a pseudo-scientific clone within a mechanism of historical embellishment.[3] The city dies of technology, censorship and money.

The city of tomorrow will not be very different to the city of today. Of course its outward appearance can vary. The metro system, the terrible blocks, mock-cultural complexes, traffic systems and housing schemes can disturb some reassuring images. But let us not be deceived: the city of today, as that of tomorrow, is a commercial commodity, disposable, 'ready-made'. In the face of this merchandise of the present, where are the people of moderation? Can one still believe in the uselessness of a smile, in bedrooms ablaze with light, in welcoming houses, in the ordinary conditions of life, in the day-to-day?

The city of today demands commitment. Urban fate does not exist. And if Paul Valéry was able to write with assurance that all civilisation is mortal, the city is in itself the guarantor of our felicities. We share the spaces of the city, but we do not know how to listen to it because the city is incredible, non-hearing; as Jean-Paul Dollé would say, who will represent the city of today?[4]

City-shelters:[5] resume a formula employed some years ago by Michel Serres, when he told us of the humble condition of his grandparents going from the land to the market and from the market to the farm in an infinite cycle of seasons. He wanted us to discover the extraordinary in the simple, but without nostalgia. Today one might take that for an excess of conservatism. But more profoundly, the author's message was simply to conceive the city in terms of its evolution, to see the value beyond the shabby affectations that hold the place of architecture. But have these thoughts on the sensitive, on the effect a place has, any chance of being heard today? We rather doubt it.

Nevertheless by looking elsewhere it seems that our ancestors have expressed the same hopes with different words. Between our pasts, located against cityscapes in our memory and the cumbersome monuments that haunt our lives,[6] the city of today has the singular place of a bride laid bare. Duchamp was right in saying that the city is a matter of dust!

History teaches us that the city is the ferment of modern civilisation. It is certainly not the museumified space, mummified and bloodless, of the urbanophiles and other apostles of the right angle.

It seems that it is impossible to talk about places without sinking into denunciation.[7] The city that surrounds us is the applied invention of urban desperation. To bandage the city is to band-aid our uncertainties. A tragic plot has fashioned the refusal of dreaming of the void, nothing, the incredible. To regiment, control, manage, normalise, regulate, to improve, to tidy, have become the key phrases of our banality. While once the 'archaeology of bricolage' was the driving force of the city,[8] nowadays we sink into a logic of the sedation of passions. *L'élégance* has fathered monsters without soul and without subtlety.

Thinking that we hush the tumult of the city we condemn it to silence. The city fossilises the useless. It preserves in its entrails objects corrupted by usage, aged by futility, magical and derisory things such as bad paving, clumsy ironwork, forgotten notices, staircases worn by centuries of use, romantic porches.

These are things that just exist and that nobody claims. Against a love for these places, indispensible in their uselessness, we are confronted with a pretence of possession.[9] The unseemly, the ugly, the disagreeable, have been laminated, reduced, crushed for the benefit of an insipid sentimentality. We ascribe

FROM ABOVE: Rue Bengali, Zones B, Europan 4, 1996; Grand Oued de Paris, Europan 4, 1996

functions to all spaces, by foolishly forgetting that the 'urban function' is merely a bureaucratic invention.

The myth of an urban requalification has become the only reply to our concerns. Enough compromises. Enough snide laughter and constructive hypocrisy. Let us allow the city to resist intentions. The luxury of the city is the uselessness of places, the sad poetry of abandoned spaces, the dust raised by the wind, the imprint of a footstep on the edge of a puddle of mud, the small tuft of grass huddled in the heat of granite paving, the stray froth surreptitiously slipped under the sterilised sign of a cheap McDonalds, the kiss of two lovers outside a crowded tram, the solitary tree against which a dog lifts his leg, the patchy reflection of the winter sun on badly repainted shutters, impressionist touches of a crowd tossed between desire and desperation, the simplicity of a grocery shop, the unseemliness of shabby paintwork. It is not the murderous light that irradiates carefully weeded public spaces. It is not the imbecility of a design panel. It is not the mediocre originality of a shop window. It is not the coarse sufficiency of the 'architect-urbanist'. It is not propriety that we need.

Who will denounce the power of those architects who bury the imagination and pretend to re-validate the urban? Who will have the courage to state that being an urbanist is not a trade but a virtue? Who will narrate the magic of abandoned places? Who will enthuse at a clump of nettles growing through the marble of a public square? Who will assert that the city is made of lovers and not of actors in some social game? Who will defend the uselessness of the wasteland? Who will carry the enthusiasm of the handyman's clutter? Who will destroy the odious streetlight?

Wanting to conceptualise the city at all costs, we subtract its humanity. The city is beautiful. It is the museum of our own history. But it is no longer ours. We assist as spectators in its metamorphosis. Everyone conspires to explain to us that it suffers and that it is necessary to heal it. But it is being made so clean, so sterilised, that one hardly dares to look at it. We cross a city that we have deconstructed of any power to move. The place no longer exists, it has become the image of the place. We celebrate the exclusion by only retaining from the city our own reflection in a shop window. Where is the enchantment in all that? Can one still dream of the spell of the city?

Our architecture sees itself as the declaration of our loves. We want a city that is available, generous, light and almost debauched, where enjoyment would have the *droit de cité*. The idea of a harmonious architecture, in the academic sense of the term, does not concern us, neither do the tricks of the avant-garde, nor displays of stylistic agility. The city and architecture cannot be represented as a built work; they act rather as the support for a narrative.

We are frightened by this city where the architecture gives itself airs of respectability in the functional sense of the term. Our sensitivity focuses rather around the banal and the ordinary, those disorderly and simple lives that are our daily environment. But our ordinariness is not the banality of making-do, the environment of denial that we all share. Our ordinariness is rare, buried, culturally despised, in the process of disappearance. It has for a long time been found in cheap districts or forgotten places; it inspires holidays and free time more than commerce and retail.

We are in search of a carnal environment, simple and real that lives directly and not through representation. We are open to all the referents and are certainly sensitive to trends of a moment. We have followed Debord, as well as Derrida. But we are not making a rhetorical reinterpretation of anything. We have never taken a semiological stance. In general, our architecture is structured by the necessary and takes its appearance from its uses.

We are a little audacious. We want a city for everyone; a hospitable city that would integrate all activities without compartmentalising them. A city that would not destroy the power of place. We want a *domopole* where the idea of urbanity resides intact. *(Translated by Tony Roch)*

Notes

1 Le Corbusier, *Urbanisme*, 1925, Flammarion (Paris), new edition 1994, p17.
2 F Choay, 'Le Règne de l'urbain et la mort de la ville', *La Ville, art et architecture en Europe 1870-1993*, exhib cat, Centre G Pompidou (Paris), 1994, pp26-35.
3 A Branzi, *Nouvelles de la métropole froide*, Centre G Pompidou (Paris), 1991.
4 J-P Dollé, 'L'Inouï urbain', Ecole des Hautes Etudes Urbaines (Lyon), 1991.
5 D Payot, *Des villes-refuges, témoignage et espacement*, Editions de l'Aube (La Tour d'Aigues), 1992.
6 See J Debord, *La Société du spectacle*, Gallimard (Paris), 1992.
7 Henri Gaudin, *Seuil et d'ailleurs*, Editions du Demi-Cercle (Paris), 1992.
8 Philippe Jarreau, *Du bricolage, archéologie de la maison*, CCI, Centre G Pompidou (Paris), 1985.
9 Clément Rosset, *Le Principe de cruauté*, Editions de Minuit (Paris), 1988.

LE K ARCHITECTURES

IN VIVO

UIA Competition, Barrio Chino, Barcelona

The competition brief required the replacing of two housing blocks with a lower density mixed-use programme comprising of 65 per cent dwellings. A new public space was to be integrated and roads were to be widened as a matter of priority. The overall site area amounts to 10,500 square metres . The area is recognisable as a district in the process of impoverishment where redundant buildings slide towards squalor. A response was required that both set a precedent and functioned within an acknowledged movement of urban redemption. Le K Architecture's scheme was shortlisted by the panel.

One of the last European working-class inner-city neighbourhoods – neither ghetto nor museum – the Barrio Chino forms part of an urban monument where authenticity still exists without being a grotesque echo of itself.

Chairs are always outside. One can sense everywhere the vibrancy of the daytime din, shouts and chatter from hair-curlers; gossip and kids yelling. Moving between loaded baskets and sedate old cigars, the narrow streets of the Barrio Chino, scorched by the elements, plunge us without warning into a world of life. Essential places are plentiful.

Yellowing *bouis-bouis* are suffused with the smell of *pulpo à la plancha* and 'tiny fried fish'. Blind alleys full of workshops, deep and heavy with secrets, merge into seediness and tiny grocery shops lined with tins and preserves, where peppers, hams and cod dry peacefully. A bar is formed by a plank and a few old wine barrels in a patch of shade.

Left over from holidays or family festivities, festoons of silver paper overflow across the balconies and mingle with the still damp washing. Venetian blinds and thick plants add the final touches of excess to facades which resemble more the layering of back gardens.

The Barrio Chino is not beautiful – it is admirable. It is not picturesque, it is

firmly anchored in a living tradition. All the qualities of a city are there at the heart of the contemporary metropolis. Nothing need be subtracted or added.

But the Barrio Chino is being corroded by decay. Even worse, it is being driven back by the pressure of 'hypo-allergenic' projects. Modernise and sanitise are the keywords. The object of the competition is clear: a necessary destruction in order to build anew, the widening of roads in order to free public space, to reinforce activities in order to promote the profitability of their functions.

Our architectural response is a dual-aspect city. The first aspect is a public, or rather, 'hyper-public' face. It is the framework for high-density living. At stake is retaining the density of minor domestic activities which make up the urban richness of the Barrio Chino. Mixing reappropriated old-fashioned elements and low-key technology, this facade stands as a replica of the original which is not formal but which reproduces existing activities. The facades retreat, the roads grow wider, but the balconies extend out to the same line. Density remains intact, the pervasive market thrives. All the apartments are conceived in such a way as to encourage the inhabitants to use their balconies as they previously did. The ground floor is completely dedicated to commercial activities or to services outlets.

The other aspect provides the benefit of a modern environment which the city of the past lacked. Bathed in light, silence, nature, coolness in summer, heat in winter; the ground is fertile here as in an orchard. This is what we call the 'bio-face'. A true urban nature reserve in which giant eucalyptus and Provençal bamboo co-exist, the bio-face is also a public place but it is intended as a place of contemplation and meditation. This area is not completely accessible; one can only cross it or stop there on a single central path bordered by orange trees. The remainder is a kind of preserved sanctuary.

in vivo, OPPOSITE, FROM ABOVE: hyperpublic face; bio-face; ABOVE: workshop alleyways

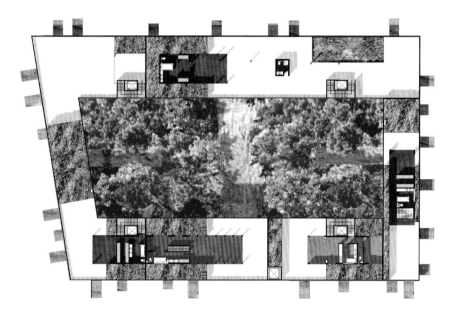

On this side, the apartments have neither balconies nor loggias. Large glazed openings maintain a direct relationship with the exterior, but even this is limited, conceived so as to restrict the interaction with the exterior. Here, nature penetrates the dwelling rather than the dwelling extending into nature.

'Home sweet home' is wedged between complex social spaces and wild nature, free yet protected. All the apartments are dual-aspect and give on to both faces, but their similarities end there. We wanted to create a popular Barrio Chino in the widest sense of the word: not a place for the poor nor exclusively middle class. Even if it is more politically correct to preach social equality in architecture, the response embodied in 'in vivo' is the reality of a society which cherishes social difference. All social classes should be represented there, so there are multiple typologies for our apartments. They range from the modest two-roomed apartment to the aristocratic duplex with terrace, swimming pool and roof garden as well as the entire spectrum in between.

In the private heart of the blocks, the tiny alleyways full of artisans existed prior to our intervention. The project retains them at the centre of the bio-face.

Small alcoves allow access to the parking areas. The operator controls the lifting platforms from a mobile cabin. This system is designed as much to eliminate endless and insalubrious ramps as to uphold the principal of inhabited parking lots.

A thermo-regulatory bioclimatic system for the bio-face consists of hot air from the upper levels being drawn into a series of straw-like tubes. Ducted to an undergound cave and cooled by running water, it ends up as a jet of steam around the bamboo. *(Translated by Tony Roch)*

FROM ABOVE: plan at level 3; roof plan; plan at level 5

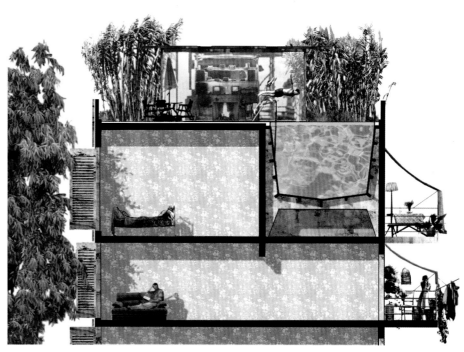

FROM ABOVE L TO R: section; aerial image; section

GÜNTER BEHNISCH
CIRCUMSTANTIAL ARCHITECTURE

From 1969 until 1972, Günter Behnisch & Partner worked on the design for the 'Olympiapark' in Munich, assisted by many employees, engineers, specialists and colleagues.

In those days everything happened very quickly and a building's programme would be developed and amended during the planning process. The situation seemed to call for a name to represent this type of work, a name that would be of assistance when it came to collaborating meaningfully with a multitude of employees and colleagues, many of whom we did not know yet. This name would have to be vague enough to allow different interpretations and developments while, at the same time, being acceptable to everyone. Eventually, we settled on the expression *Situationsarchitektur* (situational or circumstantial architecture).

After the war, Germany's building industry lacked the capacity required to construct the large number of buildings needed, as the result of either destruction or new demand. Before working on the Munich project, our reaction to this condition was to develop industrially prefabricated construction systems. A number of remarkable buildings were built utilising these systems (two examples would be the Polytechnic in Ulm and the Polytechnic in Aalen).

However, once these systems – having been developed, used and, eventually, adopted by others – were controlled by production and administrative organisations, it became apparent that they could be used as instruments of power, thus curtailing the freedom of architecture. In short, architecture was put under the control of bureaucratic institutions.

In response, we wished to recapture the freedom that had been lost. The world of architecture once more needed to be perceived as wide-ranging, diverse and colourful. *Situationsarchitektur* became our motto reminding us that design issues had to be resolved with regard to their uniqueness in terms of location and point in time. Generalisations, such as 'construction systems', constantly recurring systems of architectural styles or preconceived notions of geometric order, were to be avoided as much as possible.

Over time other concerns arose. We attempted to use construction techniques and materials that were 'non-elitist', things that were at everybody's disposal and therefore everyday. Formal, material and technical solutions were to be appropriately aligned with the tasks at hand and executed with an economy of means – definitely not too strained or excessively equipped; so that anybody would be able to afford them. Our opinion was that less sophisticated technology was preferable to highly sophisticated technology and that the form of individual objects should develop naturally according to their individual requirements – that the individual object should become 'the way it wants to be itself'. Established concepts of formal, material, geometric structures should not dominate but, instead, individual objects should come together forming a whole 'of their own free will'. Choosing the notion of collage to provide a formal framework for this approach, many things became possible – new next to old, designed next to what apparently has not been designed, long next to short, red next to blue, etc. Rightful claims, wherever they may come from, should not be rejected on the basis of 'architectural reasons'.

'Everyday architecture'; I don't know if it's everyday. Not everybody would consider it so. In the end, people only see what they are able to recognise. We take pleasure in seeing it in the way I have just outlined.

I grant that in this process problems that are not particular to architecture are dealt with, but those too are part of our architectural work. Ultimately, how we resolve these problems demonstrates the way in which we deal with our world. Objects, for instance, are treated with great brutality nowadays. People feel as if they own the world, as if they can freely make decisions about everything in it, as if they have the right to judge and condemn things. Our reaction is to place objects within our architectural landscape and carefully preserve the integrity of each. While these objects may be everyday – not necessarily beautiful and possibly re-used – the strategy for their combination is anything but everyday.

The openness inherent in this strategy is something we like. Nevertheless, openness with respect to objects, and openness towards the functional, the technical, the formal, the ecological and the economic, towards the

Behnisch & Behnisch, main administrative building of the Landesverisicherungsanstalt Schleswig-Holstein, Lübeck, 1994-97

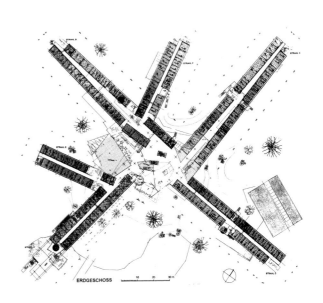

Behnisch & Behnisch, main administrative building of the Landesversicherungsanstalt Schleswig-Holstein, Lübeck, 1994-97, FROM ABOVE: axonometric; section; ground floor plan

Behnisch & Partner, Montessori School,
Ingolstadt-Hollerstauden, 1997, LEFT: plan

developer as much as the ones affected – openness also towards the everyday – has two sides. On the one hand this open-mindedness allows architecture to remain responsive, offering the opportunity to change a design strategy even at the last stage. On the other hand, it causes many people to think that they can have a say in this 'everyday architecture'. And so we cannot hide behind architecture anymore.

This type of 'open everyday architecture' facilitates our work at the office. It allows us to integrate co-workers' individual performances into our projects without forcing these (mostly young) colleagues to adhere to a specific style; the solution for the whole does not determine their solution for a part or force them to execute something originally designed by someone else. These ideas are realised in the type of work our office produces. We at the office can identify individual contributions in a finished project. Outsiders, however, tend to think that what is common to all of us dominates our buildings.

Our – and I agree with the title – 'everyday architecture' does not simply reproduce the everyday. That obviously exists as well, but not

Günter Behnisch & Partners, Extended Primary School, Lorch, 1980-82, RIGHT: plan

for us. We take almost all materials for our architecture from daily life, but we don't use them in the way one would in daily life. For example, formal aspects are derived from the realm of art, and free, light, playful aspects are derived from the realm of ideas.

Nothing is taken for granted in this process. Formal aspects are developed by wrestling with the laws of form and their development over time, the goal being to create as few new formal restraints as possible, and instead to achieve as much freedom as possible. It is important to clear a space in which things can develop freely and playfully, space in which the materials of daily life, which we tend to encounter in cramped settings, can free themselves and flourish. However, others, especially those in power, also crave this free space. Obviously defeat of their demands would be possible if architecture was to be made inaccessible through the rigorous application of a formal method. This is not for us. We would then be robbing ourselves of the things that we wish to welcome. *(Translated by Katharina Ledersteger-Goodfriend)*

1 classroom
2 hall
3 main entrance
4 biology
5 physics/chemistry
6 administration
7 teachers
8 library
9 palm court
10 arts and crafts

BIOGRAPHIES

Sarah Wigglesworth is an architectural practitioner and teacher working in London. She is currently Director of the Masters Course in Design and Theory at Kingston University and principal of her own practice, which was recently selected for the *UK New Practices Directory*. She is a founder of *Desiring Practices*, a co-organiser of the symposium, exhibitions and book of the same name (1995).

Jeremy Till is an architectural teacher and practitioner working in London. Jointly awarded the Fulbright Arts Fellowship with Sarah Wigglesworth in 1991, he is presently Senior Lecturer at the Bartlett, University College London, where he is Undergraduate Course Director. He is also Visiting Professor at the Technical University, Vienna.

Günter Behnisch is founding partner of Behnisch and Partners, one of Germany's most influential architectural practices, which has won numerous awards for its work over 45 years. The practice employs architects from all over the world who work in a collaborative and open manner. The work of Behnisch and Partner has recently been the subject of an monograph published by Academy Editions.

Phillip Hall-Patch studied at both Oxford Brookes University and The Bartlett, University College London, where he was awarded the Ambrose Poynter Prize for theory. He is currently working in practice with Mark Muir & Co, Architects & Designers.

Gillian Horn is an architect currently working in practice and running a design unit at the Architectural Association in London. Her previous work has been published in *Blueprint*, *Building Design* and *Scroope*.

Le K Architectures was formed in France in 1993. The group consists of Karine Herman, Jérôme Sigwalt, and Thierry Verdier. Their work was commended in Europan 3 and awarded first places in Cimbeton 95 and Europan 4. The group are soon to complete their first building, Le Fond Régional d'Art Contemporain, in Montpellier, France.

Patrick Keiller studied architecture and worked in several offices in the 1970s. During the 1980s he made short films and taught in art and architecture schools. His feature *London* was released in 1994 and *Robinson in Space* in January 1997.

Ben Kelly trained at Lancaster College of Art and the Royal College of Art. He established Ben Kelly Design in 1977 and since then their award-winning, innovative work has been published worldwide. The practice extends across architectural and interior projects, and their work has been widely influential in design culture.

Katharina Ledersteger-Goodfriend holds a BSc in Architecture and a MSc with Distinction in the History and Theory of Modern Architecture from the Bartlett, University College London. Preparing to teach theories of architecture and space at ArtCenter in Pasadena, she is currently living in Los Angeles.

Niáll McLaughlin was educated at University College Dublin from where he graduated in 1994. He worked for Scott Tallon Walker in Dublin and London, before setting up his own practice in London in 1991. Recent projects include houses, a monastery, a swimming pool and a competition-winning art gallery, all in London. He was named UK Young Architect of the Year in 1998.

Greil Marcus is the author of *Lipstick Traces*, *The Dustbin of History* and *Invisible Republic*, among other books. He is contributing editor at *Artforum* and writes a weekly cultural column for the *New York Times*.

Michael Marriot is one of the Britain's foremost young furniture designers. Educated at the London College of Furniture and the Royal College of Art, he has set up his own studio specialising in furniture design. He is a visiting lecturer at the RCA and Kingston University.

Samuel Mockbee is an architect and teacher resident in Mississippi. Since 1991 he has been Alumni Professor of Architecture at Auburn University, where he runs the ground-breaking Rural Studio. He has been Visiting Professor at Berkeley, Harvard, Yale, Oklahoma and North Carolina. He is also Partner in Mockbee/Coker Architects whose work has received awards and been exhibited worldwide.

Roto Architects was founded in 1991 and has developed collaborative working relationships with clients resulting in non-standard solutions to unconventional and unique projects. The practice, based in Los Angeles, has been awarded numerous awards.

Susan Nigra Snyder is a graduate of Mount Holyoke College and the University of Pennsylvania. She is an architect, practices with CoCA, Company for the Civic Arts and teaches in the Architecture and Fine Arts Department of the Graduate School of Fine Arts at the University of Pennsylvania in Philadelphia.

Clark Stevens is a principal, with Michael Rotondi, of Roto Architects, inc. Educated at the University of Michigan and Harvard University, from where he graduated with distinction, he has taught and lectured throughout the United States.

Jessica Stockholder is well known for her large-scale installations, including those at the Dia Center for Art in New York, Musée Picasso in Antibes and Musée de Beaux-Arts de Nantes. She has been awarded the John Simon Guggenheim Fellowship. Represented in numerous public collections, she has been widely published.

Rewi Thompson Ltd was established in 1983 in Auckland, New Zealand. Their work, which addresses the dramatic social, cultural and economic changes that New Zealand is encountering, has received over 16 awards and covers a broad range of building types. They have lectured and taught throughout New Zealand, and in the USA, Germany and Australia.

Åsmund Thorkildsen is Director of the Kunstnernes Hus in Oslo. Curator for the Olympic Collection 94 at Lillehammer, he is art critic for the daily *Drammens Tidende & Buskeruds Blad*. He is also Associate Professor in art theory at the National College of Art, Craft and Design in Oslo.

Nicholas Till is Senior Lecturer at Wimbledon School of Art where he runs the MA programme: Critical Studies in Visual Arts and Theatre. He is also author of *Mozart and the Enlightenment* and works as a theatre director.

Alex Wall is a graduate of the University of North Carolina and the Architectural Association. A registered architect, he has practised with the Office of Metropolitan Architecture. He is currently Professor of Urban Design, Faculty of Architecture, University (TH) of Karlsruhe, Germany.